RICHARD III

RICHARD III

FROM CONTEMPORARY CHRONICLES, LETTERS & RECORDS

Keith Dockray
&
Peter Hammond

FONTHILL

Fonthill Media Limited
Fonthill Media LLC
www.fonthillmedia.com
office@fonthillmedia.com

First published as Richard III: A Reader in History, 1988
Revised and reprinted as Richard III: A Source Book 1997
This further revised edition first published in the United Kingdom 2013

British Library Cataloguing in Publication Data:
A catalogue record for this book is available from the British Library

ISBN 978-1-78155-313-8 (print)
ISBN 978-1-78155-333-6 (e-book)

Typeset in 10pt on 13pt Sabon LT
Printed and bound in England

Connect with us

 facebook.com/fonthillmedia twitter.com/fonthillmedia

CONTENTS

PREFACE

Since this book first appeared under the title *Richard III A Reader in History* in 1988 much new work on the last Yorkist king has been published. In particular, there have been three major biographical studies: Rosemary Horrox, *Richard III —A Study of Service* (1989); Michael Hicks, *Richard III —The Man Behind the Myth* (1991); and A. J. Pollard, *Richard III and the Princes in the Tower* (1991). Also, in 1993, John Gillingham edited a collection of essays under the title *Richard III: A Medieval Kingship*.

In order to incorporate the fruits of recent scholarship, where appropriate, I have made substantial changes to my original book, including much rewriting of the commentaries, splitting the section on 'The Enigma of Richard III' into two ('Introduction: Sources and Historiography' and 'Richard III: The Man and the King'), putting in a new section on 'Richard III, France and Scotland', adding a number of extra documents, updating the bibliography and providing an index. I have also drawn considerably on my 1992 Headstart History pamphlet *Richard III*.

The documentary material is divided into sections which focus on particular aspects of Richard's life and reign. Each chapter is prefaced by a commentary providing a context for the extracts, with numbers in brackets referring to the documents which follow.

My gratitude to former colleagues and students at the University of Huddersfield remains as strong as ever, and I must now additionally thank Dr Peter Fleming, Peter Allender and students at both the University of the West of England and University of Wales College, Newport, for helping to keep my interest in fifteenth–century politics in general, and Richard III in particular, alive and kicking. Moreover, despite the very best of feline endeavours, my two delightful cats Snitch (now sadly deceased) and Snubby have not managed to prevent either the original book or this new edition being completed.

Keith Dockray
Bristol, March 1997

NOTE TO NEW EDITION

When I was asked by Keith and his publisher Alan Sutton to revise this book I was pleased to agree since I believe that it is a valuable source book for studying the life and reign of Richard III. In the years since the 1997 edition was issued there has been much new work on the king, in the past two years the site of his last battle has been settled after centuries of doubt and his burial place with his bones still present was found late last year. This book takes new work and these discoveries into account, making it invaluable for future re-evaluation of the last Plantagenet's life and reign.

Peter Hammond
June 2013

ABBREVIATIONS

Commines: Philippe de Commynes, *Memoirs: The Reign of Louis XI 1461–83*, transl. M. Jones (London, 1972)

CPR: Calendar of Patent Rolls, Edward IV, 1467–77, Edward IV–Edward V–Richard III, 1476–85 (1899, 1901)

Crowland: The Crowland Chronicle Continuations 1459–1486, ed. N. Pronay and J. Cox (Gloucester, 1986)

Fabian: R. Fabyan, *The New Chronicles of England and of France*, ed. H. Ellis (London, 1811)

Great Chronicle: The Great Chronicle of London, ed. A. H. Thomas and I. D. Thornley (1938, reprinted Gloucester, 1983)

Harleian MS 433: British Library Harleian MS 433, ed. R. Horrox and P. W. Hammond, 4 vols (Richard III Society, 1979–83)

Mancini: Dominic Mancini, *The Usurpation of Richard III*, ed. and transl. C. A. J. Armstrong (Oxford 1969, reprinted Gloucester, 1984)

More: Sir Thomas More, *The History of King Richard III*, ed. R. S. Sylvester (Complete Works, Yale edn, 11, 1963)

Paston Letters: The Paston Letters 1422–1509, ed. J. Gairdner, 6 vols (1904, reprinted Gloucester, in one volume, 1983)

Plumpton Correspondence: Plumpton Correspondence, ed. T. Stapleton (Camden Society, 1839, reprinted Gloucester, 1990)

Rolls of Parliament: Rotuli Parliamentorum, ed. J. Strachey and others, 6 vols (1767–77)

Vergil: Polydore Vergil, *Three Books of Polydore Vergil's English History*, ed. H. Ellis (Camden Society, 1844)

Vitellius AXVI Chronicles of London, ed. C. L. Kingsford (1905, reprinted Gloucester, 1977)

York Civic Records: York Civic Records, 1, ed. A. Raine (Yorkshire Archaeological Society Record Series, 1939)

INTRODUCTION

SOURCES AND HISTORIOGRAPHY

No English king has suffered wider fluctuations of reputation than Richard III, perhaps the most controversial ruler England has ever had, and none has a more fascinating historiography. Extremes of interpretation have long abounded: on the one hand, he has been vilified as a ruthless master of intrigue, a callous murderer of rivals ranging from the simple–minded Henry VI to his own innocent nephews, and a tyrannical, even wicked, ruler; on the other, he has been extravagantly praised as a man of admirable character who, given a little more time, would have proved a splendid king (perhaps, indeed, the best king England has ever had). Since its first appearance in the early 1590s, moreover, William Shakespeare's gripping play *Richard III*, as the culmination of so-called Tudor tradition deliberately denigrating the king, has rarely been far from the centre of controversy. Again, extreme positions are not difficult to find. Should we, for instance, accept the argument that Shakespeare's picture is fundamentally sound and has a solid basis in fact? Or should we, rather, reject Tudor tradition more or less in its entirety and seek to build up an altogether different portrait of the last Yorkist king?

Even in the twentieth century Richard III has found both passionate defenders and harsh critics. Although many professional historians have been inclined to play it cool, emotion has nonetheless been generated in such diverse settings as our most prestigious universities (Oxford and Cambridge), our most famous public school (Eton), the privileged benches of the House of Lords, the journalistic ranks of both national and local newspapers, and even the programme-producing fraternities of British radio and television. The 'In Memoriam' columns of the *Times*, *Guardian* and *Independent* never fail to carry at least one loving remembrance of the last Plantagenet on the anniversary of his untimely death on the battlefield of Bosworth in 1485; while, in 1984, London Weekend Television staged a four-hour mock trial of Richard III (when, predictably, a jury found the king not guilty of the murder of his nephews). Can any other English monarch, moreover, boast so determined a champion as the detective novelist Josephine Tey? In her bestselling novel *The Daughter of Time* (published in 1951), we find Miss Tey's Detective Inspector Grant, anxious to combat the tedium of enforced idleness in hospital and inspired by an early sixteenth-century portrait of Richard III, turning his investigative talents to an unorthodox use: inevitably, he ends up clearing the king of all those crimes so unjustly credited to him by the likes of Sir Thomas More and William Shakespeare and casts his successor Henry VII in the role of murderer of the Princes in the Tower. Even more strikingly, Richard's enthusiastic rehabilitators, not only in England but elsewhere, have created flourishing societies dedicated both to defend his reputation against the dastardly charges of Tudor hacks (and anyone else who would blacken his name) and praise his achievements (whether as Duke of Gloucester or as king) in the highest of terms. In America during the 1930s, indeed, the 'Friends of Richard III Incorporated' included among their ranks such distinguished figures as the writer James Thurber, the artist Salvador Dali and the legendary Hollywood movie star Tallulah Bankhead. The English 'Richard III Society', originally founded in 1924 as the 'Fellowship of the White Boar', went one better in 1980 when it enlisted as its patron the present Richard Duke of Gloucester. The society certainly continues to flourish and perform sterling service in pursuit of its proudly declared aim:

> ... to promote in every possible way research into the life and times of Richard,
> III, and to secure a re-assessment of the material relating to this period, and
> of the role in English history of this monarch.

Indeed, *The Ricardian* (quarterly journal of the society) is an important academic periodical, presenting the results of original research by amateur and professional historians alike. The 'Richard III Society' has also earned the gratitude of all fifteenth–century scholars by its sponsorship of the publication of major primary sources, most notably *British Library Harleian Manuscript 433* and a new edition/translation of the *Crowland Chronicle*.[1]

Clearly, if the historian is to have even a sporting chance of getting behind the mythology surrounding Richard III and grappling with the reality, it is to contemporary and near-contemporary records, letters and narrative histories that he must firmly address himself. And, in recent times, most new material has been gleaned from the vast bulk of surviving (and still largely unpublished) government records of later fifteenth century England. There are, unfortunately, no State Papers as such for the Yorkist age, and this seriously inhibits our understanding of the inner dynamics of Yorkist politics (as compared, for example, with the reigns of Henry VIII and Elizabeth I in the sixteenth century). Nevertheless, public records, particularly those of great departments of state like the Chancery and Exchequer, are vitally important. The Chancery Patent Rolls, for instance, provide insight into the exercise of government power in a whole range of respects and certainly constitute a rich source of information for both the nature and extent of royal patronage.[2] Similarly, that splendid register of signet letters and memoranda relating to the protectorate and reign of Richard III, familiar to historians as British Library Harleian Manuscript 433, is an invaluable guide to the behaviour of politically active men, the rewards many of them received, and the sequence of events during the turbulent years 1483–5.[3] Scholars are also increasingly making use of legal records, such as the voluminous archives of the court of King's Bench, just as they have long drawn on the Rolls of Parliament (although, regrettably, these are much less informative than the Lords and Commons journals of early modern times).[4] Borough records, too, can provide much insight into national as well as local politics and government: the York Civic Records, for instance, supply interesting data on Richard III both before and after he became king.[5]

Private letters and papers first appear in significant quantities in fifteenth-century England and have long been recognized as an important quarry of information for the era of the Wars of the Roses. Particularly valuable are the letters of three gentry families: the Pastons (a family of increasing wealth, status and influence in Norfolk), the Stonors (an old-established Oxfordshire family) and the Plumptons (a family hailing from the West Riding of Yorkshire). Reflecting the growth of literacy among country gentry and the spread of English as a written language, these vernacular letters, often precisely dated and not consciously recording events for posterity, can often provide valuable supplements to records and chronicles for English politics. Unfortunately, none of the collections has a great deal to offer the historian of Richard III. Both the volume and political interest of the Paston letters dwindles after 1471, and still more after 1479, but they do throw interesting light on the relations between Edward IV, George Duke of Clarence and Richard Duke of Gloucester in the early 1470s.[6] The Stonors were never inclined to dwell much on political events, although there is the occasional newsletter (for instance, a valuable report from London shortly before Richard of Gloucester's seizure of the throne in June 1483) and, in October 1483, Sir William Stonor became embroiled in Buckingham's rebellion and was subsequently attainted for treason.[7] Most of the Plumpton correspondence relates to the reign of Henry VII but, as Percy retainers in the 1470s and early 1480s, both Sir William Plumpton and his son Sir Robert were politically active in the north of England, and a few letters furnish evidence of northern politics and Richard of Gloucester's power in the north.[8] Among other surviving letters, perhaps three are particularly worthy of note. In August 1482, for instance, Edward IV wrote to Pope Sixtus IV, reporting favourably on his brother Richard's recent expedition into Scotland. A year later, Thomas Langton Bishop of St David's confided enthusiastic first impressions of Richard III's early behaviour as king to his friend the Prior of Christ Church, Canterbury:

He contents the people wherever he goes better than ever did any prince... I never liked the qualities of any prince as well as his; God has sent him to us for the welfare of us all.

Diego de Valera, by contrast, when writing to the Catholic monarchs of Spain (Ferdinand and Isabella) on 1 March 1486, portrayed Richard III's defeat and death at Bosworth as divine punishment for his evil deeds (not least his killing 'two nephews of his to whom the realm belonged').

Central and local government records, private letters and papers, as well as a range of non–documentary sources (portraits, buildings, artefacts), have clearly broadened and deepened our understanding of Richard III and his times, and will doubtless continue to do so. Yet historians, however much they may regret the necessity, still find themselves continually thrown back on narrative sources; moreover, given the paucity of contemporary narratives, they have no choice but to draw heavily on works written in early Tudor times. There is, in fact, only one strictly contemporary history of real substance: Dominic Mancini's *Usurpation of Richard III*. Yet even Mancini cannot be regarded as an impartial or objective source; he is critical, hostile even, to Richard III's usurpation; and he provides no coverage of the king's reign. No less partisan and no less critical of Richard III, if for different reasons, is the most nearly contemporary of the early Tudor narratives: an anonymous continuation of the *Crowland Chronicle*. Even so, this is the best source we have for Richard's protectorate, usurpation and reign. Both Mancini and the Crowland continuator suggest that, in southern England at least, the king was disliked and mistrusted in his own lifetime as an ambitious, devious and ruthless politician. Perhaps a northern chronicler would have presented a very different picture: unfortunately, no northerner chose to record Richard's history in detail or, if he did, his work has not survived.

Dominic Mancini, an Italian cleric and humanist, probably came to England in the summer or autumn of 1482 as part of a diplomatic mission, perhaps at the request of his patron Angelo Cato Archbishop of Vienne. In London throughout the turbulent months following Edward IV's death in April 1483, he was recalled to France, by Cato, shortly after Richard III's coronation on 6 July 1483; and it was at Cato's urging, seemingly, that he put together an account of recent events in England culminating in Richard's seizure of the throne:

> You have often earnestly asked me, Angelo Cato, most reverend father in God, to put in writing by what intrigues Richard the Third, who is now reigning in England, attained the high degree of kingship, a story which I had repeatedly recounted in your presence...

The resulting manuscript, 'concluded', so Mancini tells us, 'at Beaugency in the county of Orleans, 1 December 1483', thereafter disappeared for several centuries until, in 1934, it was found in the municipal library at Lille by C. A. J. Armstrong (who edited, translated and published it in 1936). As an authentic, contemporary description by an apparently detached observer who could write freely of what he had seen and learned in the spring and early summer of 1483, it has long been regarded as a source of the highest value (and an account that can be used as a yardstick against which to judge the reliability of early Tudor writers). Clearly, there is some truth in this but, in recent years, historians' confidence in Mancini has been considerably shaken. The author himself warns his patron that although:

> ... on your account I did not shrink from pains, yet I had not sufficiently ascertained the names of those to be described, the intervals of time, and the secret designs of men in this whole affair.... As a result of my concern for your requirements, I shall undoubtedly expose myself in writing to the criticism of my readers. Therefore you should not expect from me the names of individual men and places or that this account shall be complete in all details: rather shall it resemble the effigy of a man, which lacks some of the limbs, and yet an observer draws for himself a man's form.

And, at the end of his narrative, Mancini adds:

> These are the facts relating to the upheaval in this kingdom; but how he [Richard III] may afterwards have ruled, and yet rules, I have not sufficiently learnt because directly after these triumphs I left England for France, as you Angelo Cato recalled me. Therefore, farewell, and please show some mark of favour to our work, for, whatever its quality, it has been willingly undertaken on your account...

Certainly, Mancini's story of the events culminating in Richard III's usurpation is very much that of an outsider: he may well have spoken no English; he never seems to have left London and is inclined to be hazy about events and places outside the capital; his chronology is not always sound nor his account free of factual errors; and, since he was writing after his return to France, he may well have been influenced by hindsight and his desire to please his patron by telling as dramatic a story as possible. For instance, he was ignorant of the location of Richard of Gloucester's estates, he was two days out with the date of Edward IV's death, and he mistakenly placed the seizure of Richard Duke of York from sanctuary before the execution of William Lord Hastings. There is also the problem of just where he obtained his information, a subject on which he himself is irritatingly reticent. There can be little doubt that he was an eye-witness of some events in London; it is highly likely that he obtained information from fellow Italians in the capital and, probably, fellow clerics as well; he appears to have taken on board a range of conflicting (and, no doubt, confusing) rumours, although on occasion recognizing them as such; he recalled public announcements and, perhaps, had access to a source close to the council; and, when assessing favourably Richard of Gloucester's 'private life and public activities' prior to 1483 or castigating Queen Elizabeth Woodville and most of her family, he was almost certainly reflecting Richard's own propaganda in the spring of 1483. Dr John Argentine, physician to Edward V and the last of the young king's household to remain in attendance on him, is the only informant Mancini actually names and, as A. J. Pollard has convincingly argued, his own most consistent perspective on events is very much that of Edward V's entourage. Moreover, since Edwardian loyalists were the main victims of Richard of Gloucester's progress to the throne, it is not surprising that they should have been so hostile to him. Hence, perhaps, why Mancini took such a critical view of Richard's behaviour, portraying him in the weeks following Edward IV's death as a master of dissimulation, motivated by intense ambition and an 'insane lust for power', ruthlessly removing men (like William Lord Hastings) who stood in his way, and, on grounds that were dubious to say the least, depriving his nephew of the throne so that he might take the crown for himself. Nevertheless, Dominic Mancini remains an indispensable source for the events of April to July 1483.[9]

For Richard III's career as a whole, and his short reign in particular, the most important surviving narrative is the so-called second continuation of the *Crowland Chronicle*. Yet, as with Mancini, there is a question mark over its author's objectivity. Indeed, since not only is the chronicle anonymous but much of the manuscript was destroyed or badly damaged by fire in 1731 (thus forcing historians to rely more than they would otherwise wish on a published edition of 1684), this source has long aroused controversy. Although there has been some debate on the matter, the balance of likelihood is that the continuation was, as the author himself asserts, 'done and completed' at the Benedictine abbey of Crowland in Lincolnshire 'in the space of ten days, the last of which was the last day of April' 1486. The notion that it was written by a clerk in Chancery and only later found its way to Crowland (where it was transcribed and added to) is unconvincing. Even more vexed is the question of authorship. Clearly, the author was an intelligent, well-informed and probably elderly cleric who writes more in the manner of an early English humanist historian than a latter-day monastic chronicler. Equally evidently, he was a man of the world who had much inside knowledge of politics, government and diplomacy, and who had a particular interest in (and experience of) the Chancery and its officials. More specifically, as an apparently authentic marginal note indicates, 'he who compiled this history' was a doctor of canon law, a member of Edward IV's council and an envoy to Burgundy in 1471.

The most obvious candidate for authorship, perhaps, is John Russell Bishop of Lincoln. Russell was indeed a doctor of canon law and a royal councillor who was used on diplomatic missions by Edward IV; politically knowledgeable he would certainly be, since he served as Edward IV's keeper of the Privy Seal in the later 1470s and Richard III's (perhaps reluctant) chancellor 1483–85, and he is known to have been at Crowland in April 1486. Yet the case against Russell seems no less strong: the perspective of the continuation is not that of a great officer of state; if the author was indeed Richard III's chancellor, it is strange that both the quality and quantity of information for his reign is inferior to that for Edward IV's; the style of the chronicle is quite unlike Russell's known work; and, if it was written by a bishop during a visit to Crowland, it is extraordinary that the author of the next continuation was unaware of the fact. Alternatively, the second continuator may have been a member of Russell's entourage in April 1486: Richard Lavender Archdeacon of Leicester, perhaps, or the recently retired proto-notary of Chancery, Henry Sharp. Since Lavender, as a full-time diocesan official, is unlikely to have had the political knowledge necessary, Sharp seems the more likely of the two (and Nicholas Pronay makes a strong case for his authorship in his introduction to the 1986 edition/translation of the *Crowland Chronicle*). Although a doctor of civil (not canon) law, as a high-ranking Chancery official Sharp would probably have known Russell well, frequently attended council meetings and had the knowledge of political, administrative and diplomatic affairs under Edward IV so clearly displayed in the continuation; his career seems to have been in decline under Richard III (perhaps helping to explain both the lessening of detail and the tone of hostility to Richard); and he had virtually retired (at the age of about sixty-six) by April 1486. Nevertheless, as Pronay concludes, 'we have no direct evidence whatsoever' that Sharp was the second continuator and the author must therefore remain 'the Great Anonymous of our historiography'. What really matters, anyway, is that the author, whoever he was, is both well informed about Yorkist politics and notably critical of Richard III. Despite his claim to be writing 'without any conscious introduction of falsehood, hatred or favour' insofar as 'the true course of events was known to us', he is partisan in his approach to Richard, regarding him as a master of deceit and duplicity. Even before 1483 he comments adversely on Richard's conduct during an expedition to Scotland in 1482 and, although he obviously regarded the Woodvilles (Edward IV's relatives by marriage) as a pernicious influence in politics, he did not approve of the execution of Hastings, regarded Richard's northern connection as alien and undesirable, and deeply disapproved of his seizure of the throne. The chronicler's treatment of the king's reign is generally hostile as well, not least his scathing comments on Richard's behaviour in connection with the illness and death of his wife (early in 1485), his excessive financial exactions and the tyranny of the northern dominated regime which, he believed, Richard III established in southern England. Perhaps most telling of all is his treatment of Bosworth and the accession of Henry VII: here, surely, is clear evidence that, even as early as April 1486, the new Tudor king's hostile propaganda against his predecessor was beginning to make its mark. During the night before the battle, he tells us, Richard III was reported to have seen 'in a terrible dream a multitude of demons apparently surrounding him'; as for Bosworth itself:

> In the end a glorious victory was granted by heaven to the Earl of Richmond, now sole king, together with the priceless crown which King Richard had previously worn... [The] new prince [soon] began to receive praise from everyone as though he was an angel sent from heaven through whom God deigned to visit his people and to free them from the evils which had hitherto afflicted them beyond measure.[10]

Certainly, during the reigns of the first two Tudors there did develop a powerful tradition of the Tudor dynasty as the saviour of England from the chaos and confusion of the Wars of the Roses in general and the tyranny of Richard III in particular. Neither Henry VII nor Henry VIII seems to have had a deliberate policy of mounting a full-scale propaganda campaign against Richard III designed to blacken his name and, as Alison Hanham has argued, much that is commonly described as Tudor bias against Richard 'may in reality derive from the urge to tell a good story'. Nevertheless, 1485 did tend to be portrayed by Polydore Vergil, Edward Hall and their successors as a turning-point in English history, with Henry VII cast as the inaugurator of a 'brave new world' and Richard III (as Henry's immediate predecessor and the king whom he defeated at Bosworth) the victim of ever-increasing denigration. Tudor writers, moreover, had a solid basis of contemporary southern hostility to Richard on which to build, as Dominic Mancini had demonstrated in his narrative of 1483; the Crowland continuator, in April 1486, portrayed Henry VII as a dynastic peacemaker; and the first Tudor certainly did promulgate propaganda presenting himself in the role of England's deliverer from tyranny. Even before his invasion of August 1485, indeed, Henry is on record describing Richard III as 'that homicide and unnatural tyrant'; while, soon after he took the throne, he condemned his predecessor as 'the enemy of nature' and, in his first parliament, as responsible for the 'shedding of infants' blood'. Interestingly, too, some commentators contradicted, after 1485, what they had written before. A visiting Italian humanist Pietro Carmeliano, for instance, praised Richard III in 1484 as an outstandingly pious, modest, munificent and just ruler; yet two years later, after he had entered the service of Henry VII, Carmeliano condemned Richard no less vigorously as the villainous murderer of Henry VI and the Princes in the Tower. The Warwickshire antiquary John

Rous, in the so-called Rous Roll (a history of the earls of Warwick) written during the reign of Richard III, praised the king in notably extravagant terms, as a man who ruled his realm 'full commendably' and thereby earned 'the love of all his subjects, rich and poor'. Following Henry VII's accession, however, not only did Rous make strenuous efforts to suppress his earlier commendation of Richard but also, in his *History of the Kings of England* (written shortly before his death in 1491), penned a vociferously hostile portrait of the king as the unnatural product of two years in his mother's womb, 'emerging with teeth and hair to his shoulders', a man who 'like a scorpion combined a smooth front and a stinging tail' and ruled 'in the way Antichrist is to reign'. Even in his *History*, though, Rous commended Richard as a builder and a patron, a man who, early in his reign, refused offers of money from London, Gloucester and Worcester 'affirming that he would rather have their love than their treasure', and a king who, on the battlefield at Bosworth, 'bore himself like a gallant knight [and] honourably defended himself to his last breath'.[11] A Welsh poet, writing about the same time, omitted even these mitigating characteristics: for Dafydd Llwyd, Richard was a Saracen, 'a little ape', who committed the 'sin of Herod' in destroying his nephews (as well as deliberately killing several lords of the realm). Bernard Andre, in similar vein, as the official historiographer of Henry VII writing at the end of the century, deliberately contrasted his splendidly upright patron with the monstrous Richard III who, delighting only too clearly in his own evil deeds, 'swollen with rage like a serpent that has fed on noxious herbs... roars a wild command to his soldiers [at Bosworth] that he may slay Richmond himself with new and unheard-of tortures'. On the Continent, meanwhile, the shrewd Burgundian commentator Philippe de Commines' informants at the French court (who may well have included the exiled Henry Tudor himself and certainly some of his followers) convinced him that Richard III was indeed an arrogant, cruel and ruthless man who was justly deprived of the throne by God's chosen agent Henry Tudor Earl of Richmond. 'Should one describe this as Fortune?', Commines asks rhetorically: 'Surely it was God's judgement'.[12]

The most significant development in historical writing in fifteenth-century England came in London with the compilation of a series of civic narrative histories known collectively as the London chronicles. Three of these, all put together during Henry VII's reign, closely inter-connected and clearly influenced by the climate of opinion then prevailing, are of value for Richard III: *Vitellius AXVI*, the *New Chronicles of England and of France* and the *Great Chronicle of London*. Although unfortunately both anonymous and the least detailed of the three, *Vitellius AXVI* was probably compiled earlier than the others (in the 1490s). The *New Chronicles* and the *Great Chronicle*, so scholars now believe, were probably written by the same man: Robert Fabian, citizen, alderman and sheriff of London in 1493–94, who died in 1513 and was actually living in the capital during the years 1483–85. The *New Chronicles* are often known, indeed, as *Fabian's Chronicle* (and Fabian was specifically credited with their authorship in the second edition of 1533), but it is the *Great Chronicle* which is both most interesting and most valuable for the usurpation and reign of Richard III. Unfortunately, it is both relatively brief and has many faults, including errors of chronology, mistakes of fact, contradictions and a tendency to take on board rumours too credulously. In particular, it may well be unduly coloured by anti-Ricardian sentiment current in early Tudor London: for instance, the chronicler accused the king of hypocrisy (not least by exhorting his subjects to behave morally while signally failing to do so himself) and concluded that he died 'with dishonour as he that sought it' and, as a result, 'now his fame is decried and dishonoured'. Nevertheless, the author of the *Great Chronicle* does seem to have some first-hand knowledge of the events he describes and certainly cannot be dismissed as a mere retailer of Tudor prejudice against Richard III.[13]

Nor, for that matter, can the Italian humanist Polydore Vergil. Vergil, a fully-fledged Renaissance historian of real quality who was obviously much influenced by his classical studies, firmly believed that history 'displays eternally to the living those events which should be an example and those which should be a warning'. Encouraged to write his *English History* by Henry VII, he dedicated the completed work to Henry VIII, and his treatment of Richard III (the most comprehensive available to us) clearly reflects the sources of information accessible to him (often hostile to the king). Evidently, he consulted many men who could remember well back into the Yorkist period (probably including some who had played a prominent part in Yorkist politics), showed himself nicely aware of conflicting interpretations, genuinely attempted to distinguish fact from fiction, and firmly sought to establish the relationship between cause and effect. Additionally, he had access to a considerable range of written materials (including one or more London chronicles and, perhaps, the text of the second Crowland continuator). Although no official hack and prepared to admit that Richard III had *some* good qualities (notably courage), he did, however, incline to interpret English history in favour of the Tudors and must certainly be regarded as one of the major architects of later Tudor tradition about Richard: in particular, as Charles Ross has emphasized, he employed a veritable 'smear technique' when considering the king's psychology and motivation, 'constantly suggesting elements of deceit and dishonesty behind the façade of an outwardly correct and apparently well-intentioned public behaviour'. As soon as he heard of Edward IV's death, Vergil tells us, Richard 'began to be kindled with an ardent desire of sovereignty' and determined thereafter 'to accomplish his purposed spiteful practice by subtlety and sleight'; subsequently, 'being blind with covetousness of reigning whom no foul fact could now hold back', he seized the throne 'without assent of the commonalty' and did so 'contrary to the law of God and man', and, given the fact that Richard 'thought of nothing but tyranny and cruelty', at the finish God gave victory at Bosworth to Henry VII.[14]

Even more influential than Vergil in establishing Richard III's reputation as an evil tyrant was Sir Thomas More. More's *History of King Richard the Third*, written (in English and Latin concurrently) in the early part of Henry VIII's reign but mysteriously abandoned unfinished and unrevised by its author, provides far more detail than Vergil on Richard's character, behaviour and the sequence of events from April to October 1483. Yet this source is fraught with controversy: its modern editor R. S. Sylvester, for instance, believed More's portrait very much reflected the historical image of Richard current in the early sixteenth century; Alison Hanham would have us regard the *History* as literature rather than as 'a work of scholarship embodying the results of historical research' and, in 1975, was inclined to classify it as an elaborate 'historical drama in five acts'; and, recently, P. W. Hammond has dismissed it as 'little more than a treatise against tyranny, with Richard of Gloucester as the exemplar of the tyrant'. Richard III's modern rehabilitators have certainly been inclined to pour scorn on More's *History*: it is indeed doubtful, they argue, if More saw himself writing history at all; he was composing the work many years after the king's death and can have had no first-hand knowledge (while some of his informants, such as Cardinal John Morton, had no reason to speak well of Richard); he is frequently inaccurate, often prepared to embellish his narrative for dramatic effect (about a third of it consists of invented speeches) and always overwhelmingly concerned to portray Richard as a grand villain. The *History* clearly is very dramatic and More undoubtedly was preoccupied with tyranny (which he detested) when writing it: Richard III as a usurping tyrant dominates his narrative and many of the leading elements in Tudor tradition—including the king's monstrous appearance, his murder of Henry VI, his engineering the death of Clarence, his plotting for the crown long before Edward IV's death, his master-minding the murder of the Princes in the Tower and the invariable infamy of his motives—either first appear or are first fully developed here. Yet it must always be borne in mind that there was no shortage of men in the political circles in which More moved who could provide him with inside information; his reliance on classical models (like Tacitus and Sallust) may go far to explain many of his dramatic devices (his comparison of the 'good' King Edward IV and the 'bad' King Richard III, for instance, is strongly reminiscent of Tacitus' contrast of the Emperors Augustus and Tiberius); he probably had access to London chronicles and the manuscript of his fellow Renaissance scholar Polydore Vergil; he was not writing to please any particular patron; and, despite the all too obvious loading of the dice against his villain, More did on occasion attempt to distinguish between rumour and fact. All in all, historians should give at least serious consideration to the possibility that More's basic characterizations and storyline (once shorn of his dramatic elaborations) are not only plausible but even convincing, especially since they are already mapped out to a very significant extent in earlier narratives (even Dominic Mancini's contemporary account).[15]

As the Tudor period unfolded, so did the unsavoury reputation of Richard III solidify in the pages, successively, of Edward Hall, Richard Grafton and Raphael Holinshed until, finally, it was immortalized in William Shakespeare's splendid play. Edward Hall, a staunch Protestant and ardent supporter of the Tudor dynasty, certainly drew heavily on Vergil and More in his *Union of the Two Noble Families of Lancaster and York* (published in 1548), not least in his description of Richard III personally. More than that he both added to and deepened the hostile portrait bequeathed to him, and his Richard, an out-and-out monster and tyrant, fully deserved his fate at the hands of that agent of divine providence Henry VII whose 'godly matrimony' (in taking Elizabeth of York as his queen) at last brought 'the final end to all dissensions, titles and debates' which had so long afflicted the country:

> Thus ended this prince his mortal life with infamy and dishonour, which never preferred fame or honesty before ambition, tyranny and mischief. And if he had continued still protector, and suffered his nephews to have lived and reigned, no doubt but the realm had prospered, and he much praised and beloved as he is now abhorred.[16]

The Elizabethan chroniclers Richard Grafton and Raphael Holinshed took over Hall's interpretation virtually in its entirety: Holinshed, indeed, only rarely rises above the level of plagiarism, happily lifting great chunks from the earlier works of More and Hall and incorporating them into his own narrative. William Shakespeare, seemingly, read both Hall and Holinshed and, since the playwright was rarely more faithful to his sources, his portrayal of the last Yorkist king (in the early 1590s) represents the magnificent dramatic climax of almost a century of growing denigration. What Shakespeare added to the mix, of course, was genius and, as a result, the Tudor historians' ambitious, ruthless tyrant became the Elizabethan dramatist's first great villain. Not only does the king dominate *Richard III*, moreover, he threatens to take over *3 Henry VI* as well and, more often than not, he is both an evil ruthless plotter and a man who takes a positive delight in his own wickedness. Throughout, Shakespeare makes the most of his physical deformity since, in the plays, his monstrous appearance is very much an outward manifestation of the king's warped character: physically, he is the 'crook-back', the 'foul misshapen stigmatic', the 'elvish-marked, abortive rooting hog', the 'bottled spider' and the 'poisonous hunch-backed toad'; while, temperamentally, he is 'the dreadful minister of Hell' who, having 'neither pity, love nor fear', can 'smile and murder while I smile'. No wonder, since Shakespeare's portrait of Richard III (as not only evil but witty with it) is so devastating, Tudor tradition and the popular view of the last Plantagenet king have become virtually synonymous.[17]

Even before the end of the sixteenth century, however, doubts were beginning to be expressed. William Camden in his monumental *Britannia* (published in 1586), for instance, while recording that Richard 'inhumanly murdered his nephews' and usurped the throne, nevertheless reported that 'in the opinion of the wise he is reckoned in the number of bad men but of good princes'; Camden's contemporary John Stow, even more positively, not only remarked that Richard's responsibility for the murder of his nephews was unproven but also that old men (who had seen the king) had told him that, although low in stature, he was not deformed; and, towards the end of Elizabeth's reign, there was already circulating Sir William Cornwallis's *Brief Discourse in Praise of King Richard the Third* (although, in fact, this seems to have been merely a rhetorical exercise in defence of the indefensible!). The first full-scale defence of Richard III came from the pen of Sir George Buck, Master of the Revels to James I, in the early seventeenth century: Buck's *History of King Richard the Third*, indeed, can be regarded as the prototype for modern revisionism, not least in seeking to present a northern view of Richard III. Convinced that 'all King Richard's guilt is but suspicion' and determined 'to rescue him entirely from these wrongs', Buck, a conscientious antiquarian-cum-historian who consulted a range of manuscripts (including the second continuation of the *Crowland Chronicle*), produced the first comprehensive assault on Tudor tradition and concluded that the king's 'good name and noble memory' had, indeed, been foully maligned. Certainly, Buck not only praised Richard's courage, fortitude, magnanimity, justice and piety but also pointed out that:

> ...even his adversaries and calumniators confess that he was a very wise and a prudent and politic and an heroical prince.[18]

During the seventeenth and eighteenth centuries, in fact, Richard III found both critics and defenders. Michael Drayton, in 1613, regarded him as 'this most vile devourer of his kind' and Sir Walter Raleigh, the following year, dismissed him as 'the greatest monster in mischief of all that forwent him'; Francis Bacon in 1621, although expressing a cautious scepticism about the Tudor saga and allowing that Richard had good as well as bad qualities, nevertheless believed that he was exceptionally prone to ambition, deceit and even wickedness; and over a century later, in 1762, David Hume saw no reason to question either the 'singular magnanimity, probity and judgement' of Sir Thomas More or the even more hostile judgements of Hall and Holinshed, and concluded that Richard was 'hump-backed and had a very disagreeable visage' (his body being, in fact, 'in every particular no less deformed than his mind'). Richard's defenders included William Winstanley who, in 1684, declared:

> ...as honour is always attended on by envy, so hath this worthy prince's fame
> been blasted by malicious traducers who, like Shakespeare in his play on him,
> render him dreadfully black in his actions, a monster by nature, rather than a
> man of admirable parts.

The French lawyer and Huguenot refugee Paul Rapin de Thoyras, in the early
eighteenth century, was no less critical of certain aspects of the Tudor saga,
notably the traditional story of the murder of Prince Edward of Lancaster by
Richard of Gloucester and other lords following the battle of Tewkesbury in
1471. Nevertheless, he did accept much of it: Richard III, a basically good man
sadly corrupted by ambition, certainly earned the nickname 'crookback' in his
view 'because he was so in reality'. Perhaps the best known and most influential
of all defences of the last Plantagenet king is Horace Walpole's *Historic Doubts
on the Life and Reign of Richard III* (published in 1768). Although no scholar,
Walpole combined a lively style and superficially plausible line of argument,
firmly pointed out fundamental weaknesses and inconsistencies in sixteenth-
century portrayals of Richard, and concluded that many of the crimes attributed
to the king were not only improbable but contrary to his own interests and
clearly at odds with what can definitely be deduced about his character.
Walpole's loathing for Henry VII, however, and his perverse insistence that
Perkin Warbeck (nominal leader of a major rebellion against the first Tudor)
was indeed the younger son of Edward IV, hardly inspire confidence:

> ...Henry [VII's] character, as we have received it from his own apologists, is
> so much worse and more hateful than Richard's, that we may well believe
> Henry invented and propagated by far the greater part of the slanders against
> Richard... I know not what to think of the death of Edward the Fifth: I can
> neither entirely acquit Richard of it, nor condemn him.... For the younger
> brother, the balance seems to incline greatly on the side of Perkin Warbeck,
> as the true duke of York...

Moreover, in 1793, he retracted his earlier doubts, declaring:

> I must now [in the context of the excesses of the French Revolution,
> presumably] believe that any atrocity may have been attempted or practised
> by an ambitious prince of the blood aiming at the crown in the fifteenth
> century.[19]

The Romantic revival of the early nineteenth century brought with it both
a pronounced penchant and admiration for the Middle Ages and a more

scholarly approach to historical evidence: the reputation of Richard III, however, continued to fluctuate markedly. The Roman Catholic John Lingard (in 1819), anxious to reinstate Sir Thomas More as a genuine seeker after truth, inevitably ended up condemning 'that monster in human shape' Richard III as 'a prince of insatiable ambition who could conceal the most bloody projects under the mask of affection and loyalty'. Four years later Sharon Turner, a careful scholar and historian of distinction who consulted an impressive range of original sources (including *Harleian Manuscript 433*), penned a notably moderate and even balanced survey of the king as very much a product of his age. Richard III, he concluded, 'proceeded to the usurpation of the crown with the approbation of most of the great men, both of the church and state, then in London'. Nevertheless, Turner had clear reservations about his 'treasonable and immoral action' even if 'the protector, however bad or blameable, was no worse than the most distinguished men of his day'; moreover, while clearing Richard of many crimes, he did believe the king was responsible for the murder of the Princes in the Tower.[20] Caroline Halsted, too, drew on a massive range of record material (and printed some of it) for her two-volume biography of *Richard III as Duke of Gloucester and King of England* (published in 1844). Unfortunately, as well as possessing a romantic style of writing that frequently renders her work virtually unreadable, she became a victim of her own determined revisionism and her characterization of Richard III borders on hagiography. For her, the king's 'shining abilities, his cultivated mind, his legislative wisdom, his generosity [and] his clemency' were beyond question; his seizure of the throne could be justified by his rare talents and ability for government, and he did not murder his nephews. Indeed, Halsted concluded:

> A close examination into the earliest records connected with his career will prove that, among all the heavy and fearful charges which are brought against him, few, if any, originate with his contemporaries.... Time [and] the publication of contemporary documents have made known many redeeming qualities, have furnished proof of eminent virtue, and certified to such noble exemplary deeds as already suffice to rescue King Richard's memory from at least a portion of the aggravated crimes which have so long rendered his name odious, and inspired great doubts as to the truth of other accusations which rest on no more stable authority.[21]

Later Victorian historians, while rightly praised for frequently setting new high standards of scholarship and research (particularly into the public records of later medieval England), nevertheless tended to be critical of Richard III primarily on the basis of early Tudor narratives: the king was prone to be portrayed, indeed, as the archetypal wicked uncle who mercilessly removed (by murder if necessary) rivals or opponents who stood between him and the throne and a man who could not easily be acquitted of the deeply repugnant charge of tyranny. John Richard Green, for instance, in his hugely successful *Short History of the English People* (first published in 1874) pictured Richard III as ambitious, ruthless, pitiless and, when he deemed it necessary, prepared to throw off any pretence of constitutional rule: even so, he concluded that Richard, although a bad man, might yet be judged a good king.[22] In his *Constitutional History of England* (1878), Bishop William Stubbs certainly allowed that Richard was a man of great ability, popular in the north of England prior to his accession, brave, resolute, clear-sighted and often badly served by hostile sources: yet he was also cunning, unscrupulous, 'amenable to no instincts of mercy or kindness', and never 'rid himself of the entanglements under which he began to reign' or 'cleared his conscience from the stain which his usurpation and its accompanying cruelties brought upon him'.[23] James Gairdner, a prolific scholar, a prodigious editor (of both chronicles and records) and a good narrative historian, published his *History of the Life and Reign of Richard the Third* in 1878 as well: he emerged from his very extensive researches, moreover, convinced of 'the general fidelity of the portrait [of Richard] with which we have been made familiar by Shakespeare and Sir Thomas More'. Indeed, declared Gairdner:

> The scantiness of contemporary evidences and the prejudices of original authorities may be admitted as reasons for doubting isolated facts, but can hardly be expected to weaken the conviction—derived from Shakespeare and tradition as much as from anything else—that Richard was indeed cruel and unnatural beyond the ordinary measure even of those violent and ferocious times.

Richard III, even if not an out-and-out monster, certainly was a profoundly self-interested, dissimulating and ruthless villain.[24] Gairdner, it is clear, put too much trust in the validity of Tudor tradition as a guide to the character and behaviour of Richard III: Sir Clements R. Markham, on the contrary, most vehemently rejected it! Crossing swords with Gairdner in the pages of the *English Historical Review* in 1891 on the vexed issue of the Princes in the Tower (where Markham proved an enthusiastic advocate of Henry VII's responsibility, Gairdner equally convinced of Richard III's culpability), Markham went on to produce (in 1906) the most fervent and thorough vindication of Richard III there has ever been. Clearing Richard of all crimes and in effect turning Tudor tradition on its head, Markham declared vehemently that Gairdner's Richard III defies belief:

> Such a monster is an impossibility in real life. Even Dr Jekyll and Mr Hyde are nothing to it.

Markham's own Richard is whiter than white: before becoming king he 'displayed brilliant courage as a knight and remarkable ability as a general', as well as being justly popular throughout the country' and 'beloved in Yorkshire'; once on the throne he soon demonstrated great administrative ability, vigorously suppressed insurrections, pursued a wise and judicious foreign policy, and 'anxiously sought the welfare of his people'. All the evidence against the king, Markham believed, is tainted, and the real Richard, properly rescued from 'the accumulated garbage and filth of centuries of calumny', turns out to be one of the best rulers England has ever had: the great villain, for Markham, was the cold, cunning and merciless Henry VII.[25]

Even in the twentieth century romantic revisionism has continued to make its mark, if only in the annals of over-enthusiastic amateur historians. Professional academics, by and large, have displayed considerable caution, not only rejecting the excesses of Sir Clements R. Markham but also the over-reliance by James Gairdner on hostile Tudor tradition. Among the ranks of amateur zealots, Philip Lindsay is perhaps best known. Over the top he certainly goes, most dramatically in his study of *King Richard III* (published in 1933). Firmly addressing the memory of the king, as 'the kind of man whom we should turn to now that we move trembling towards the abyss of the future', he declared emotionally that:

> ...destiny could not break [his] spirit, the spirit that is England. Nothing could destroy that spark that Richard carried in his breast, the spark that kept him fighting, struggling on, when he could see nothing but blackness ahead. Indomitable, heroic and lovable, the great Richard, last of our English kings.[26]

The twentieth-century professional historian most sympathetic to Richard III, perhaps, has been A. R. Myers: he certainly stressed, in 1954, Richard's conspicuous loyalty to his brother Edward IV, his popularity in the north, his bravery in campaign and, as king, his efforts to suppress disorder and promote justice, his financial reforms, his concern for clerical privileges, his building of churches, his advocacy of morality and his patronage of learning.[27] Paul Murray Kendall, too, in a popular yet well-researched biography published in 1955, can be regarded as a semi-professional defender of the king (Kendall was an American professor of English literature), despite a pronounced penchant for passages of purple prose and a tiresome tendency towards imaginative reconstruction in the face of inadequate evidence. In the course of 'a mere eighteen months crowded with cares and problems', Kendall concluded, Richard III:

...laid down a coherent programme of legal enactments, maintained an
orderly society, and actively promoted the well-being of his subjects ...
Richard seems to have emerged from an earlier world.... He had in him
something of the first martyrs and something of the Germanic chieftain....
If we cannot see his portrait clearly, we can at least choose its painter—not
Holbein or even Rembrandt, but perhaps El Greco.[28]

The most damning verdict on Richard III by a professional historian has
probably been put in by A. L. Rowse: his professionalism is well disguised,
however, in *Bosworth Field and the Wars of the Roses* (1966), where he took
on board Tudor tradition more or less in its entirety, compared Richard with
Adolf Hitler, and found highly questionable parallels between Richard's
government and that prevailing in Germany under Nazi rule![29]

Not until 1981 did a new and thoroughly scholarly biography of Richard
III appear, from the pen of Charles Ross (who had already, in 1974, published
a definitive study of Richard's elder brother Edward IV). Ross's Richard was,
in many respects, a strikingly conventional later medieval prince, but he was
also very much a product of the violent and ruthless era of the Wars of the
Roses. He shared to the full the delight of his age in luxury and display, his
court was lively and impressive, and he was an enthusiastic patron of building.
Professing a piety that was as sincere as it was considerable, he made a number
of religious foundations, promoted learned men to high ecclesiastical office
and proved himself a firm protector of the church. Yet his political behaviour
certainly left much to be desired. He employed character assassination as a
deliberate instrument of policy; he frequently and violently denounced his
enemies (especially the Woodvilles and Tudor partisans) for their vices and
debauchery; and he publicly humiliated his brother's former mistress Elizabeth
('Jane') Shore. His seizure of the crown in June 1483 was in fact, and was
widely seen to be at the time, 'an unashamed bid for personal power': the
political nation in general had no desire to see young Edward V removed from
the throne, still less murdered in the Tower of London (that Edward V and his
brother were indeed murdered, and in 1483, and on Richard III's orders, Ross
considered highly likely). The cardinal fact in Richard's reign, he argued, was
the urgent need to attract support, for never had a king 'usurped the throne
with so narrow a basis of support from the nobility as a whole or with so
little popular enthusiasm'. Richard III, indeed, was dangerously dependent
on his northern connection; Buckingham's rebellion demonstrated only too
clearly the degree of resentment and distrust of his regime felt throughout
the southern counties of the realm; and, after its collapse, the need to win
enhanced backing assumed the character of a race against time. Certainly,
he did make an all-out effort to secure committed support, particularly
among the nobility, and he enjoyed considerable success in this (as is shown

by the impressive turn-out for him at Bosworth). An ambitious and ruthless politician he undoubtedly was, but he was also an effective political operator who, having usurped the throne, disposed of his nephews and crushed a major rebellion, perhaps came nearer than is often allowed to establishing himself and his northern connection permanently in the corridors and places of power in fifteenth-century England.[30]

Two years after the publication of Charles Ross's biography, the Tudor saga was back with a vengeance in Desmond Seward's popular treatment of the king. Unashamedly hostile to his subject, Seward found Richard guilty of virtually every crime ever attributed to him and interpreted practically every event to his discredit (frequently in defiance of the evidence). Indeed, he proudly proclaimed:

> This is the most hostile life of Richard III to appear for over a century ... [The king] possessed the qualities of an Italian tyrant. He was the most terrifying man ever to occupy the English throne, not excepting his great nephew Henry VIII. His short life was filled by intrigue and slaughter [and if] certainly not a monster [he was] a peculiarly grim young English precursor of Machiavelli's Prince.[31]

Colin Richmond, in 1986, brought in a typically iconoclastic, as well as notably critical, assessment of the king, as *'the* wicked uncle' whose sheer audacity 'left experienced politicians gasping'. At Stony Stratford on 30 April 1483 he took Anthony Woodville Earl Rivers 'entirely by surprise'; William Lord Hastings, on 13 June, was likewise taken completely unawares; and Richard's usurpation, a few days later, came as a shock to everyone. As for the much-rumoured fate of the Princes in the Tower, it played a major role in bringing about the king's well-deserved defeat and death at Bosworth:

> Unconventional as Richard's moves were in the usurpation, which was for that very reason successful as conventional politicians were swept aside in stunned disbelief, the culminating and most unconventional of the series [the disappearance of the Princes in the Tower] had repercussions far beyond the political world in Westminster and the home counties. Although Richard, when he put down the rising of October 1483, may have thought that world had been conquered, it was the wider one of English provincial politics which, so to speak, conquered him at Bosworth. Even the lukewarmness of his northerners, manifest at Bosworth, may have had its origin in what he had done or was held to have done to the Princes.[32]

Charles Wood in 1988, by contrast, firmly rejected the notion that Richard of Gloucester, in the months following Edward IV's death, proved himself a calculating politician who systematically pursued his own perceived self-interest. Rather, he portrayed Richard as a man lacking in political foresight, ever moving from 'one unexpected crisis to the next', and following a notably 'blundering path' to regality. For several weeks in the spring of 1483 his goals seem to have been distinctly limited as he strove to keep his options open, but he did have every reason to fear the Woodvilles and his legitimate expectation of an enduring high-profile political role as Edward V's uncle was by no means assured. Before the seizure and execution of William Lord Hastings on 13 June, however, there is little evidence that Richard had decided to depose his nephew; rather, despite his tactical skill in gaining custody of Edward V at Stony Stratford on 30 April:

> ... nothing in the record of the next month and a half suggests a man of much political finesse or sagacity. Far from dominating the situation, Richard appears to have been trapped by it, uncertain what his next move should be. [Each] option appears to have been grasped on the spur of the moment, with inadequate regard for its effectiveness or likely political consequences.

Perhaps the discovery that Hastings was involved in a conspiracy against him finally triggered Richard's regal ambitions but, even in the days that followed, there was a good deal of uncertainty and confusion (for instance, regarding the grounds on which he might most convincingly claim the throne) until, at last, he became King Richard III on 26 June. Nor did his political acumen develop notably over the next two years: during his early weeks on the throne he lived in a fool's paradise, the rebellion of October 1483 took him completely by surprise, and, in 1485, he had no choice but to abandon the foolish project of marrying his own niece. On the battlefield of Bosworth, moreover, Richard:

> ... died very much as he had lived: blindly unrepentant, fittingly unshriven, and in a characteristically dramatic charge. It was but the last of his bold and impetuous gambles, a desperate attempt to win back a kingdom that he knew was on the verge of being lost.[33]

Rosemary Horrox, in 1989, deliberately eschewed matters—like Richard III's personality and the fate of his nephews—which have so often formed the enigmatic battleground between the king's denigrators and defenders. Instead, she concentrated attention on royal patronage and the role of the king's servants during the turbulent years of his high profile career. As Duke of Gloucester, she concluded, Richard proved himself 'the effective and trusted servant of his brother Edward IV' *c.* 1471–83 and 'their relationship is a copy-book example of the mutual advantages of good lordship': his rule of the north during these years was notably successful, he built up a powerful affinity there, and his loyalty to the crown was beyond reproach. Yet his interests were never exclusively northern and, as constable and admiral of England, he was consistently active on the national stage. When he seized the throne in 1483 he did so 'not from outside the prevailing political structure but from its heart' and what is most notable about his protectorate and early months as king is the degree of continuity with his brother's regime. Of course he was ambitious, obviously enjoyed the exercise of power, chose to dictate events following his brother's death, and eventually took the throne in late June 1483 (even though the protectorate was still viable): indeed, he engineered his progress to the throne by a series of pre-emptive strikes which shook the Yorkist establishment to its very foundations and rendered it powerless to resist him. The critical turning-point in his fortunes, however, was Buckingham's rebellion in the autumn of 1483, when his brother's men deserted him in droves and Henry Tudor Earl of Richmond first emerged as a serious rival. The continuity of service was now irrevocably broken and he had no choice but to reassert royal authority virtually from scratch. Moreover, although the king made very considerable efforts to widen the basis of his support in 1484–85 (and never swamped the south of England with northerners), he was forced, in practice, more and more into dependence on his still overwhelmingly north country affinity. Consequently, at Bosworth (a battle which 'should have been fought in October 1483'), he was backed very largely by the same men who had brought him to power. He certainly needed a decisive victory but, while coming very close to success, he failed in the end, and his own death on the field made the accession of Henry VII inevitable. Richard III 'destroyed the house of York', Horrox concluded, and he also 'destroyed himself': the Tudor chronicler Edward Hall was 'surely right to see his reign as a tragedy'.[34]

Two years after the appearance of Rosemary Horrox's fine monograph, Michael Hicks published a characteristically provocative study, *Richard III: The Man Behind the Myth*. He judged the king to be an able, intelligent, well-organized man, a natural leader who was loyal and generous to his retainers as well as possessing a good deal of personal charm, and a well-read, sincerely religious patron of learning and the Church. Neither a cripple nor incapable of bearing arms, he could, when it suited him, prove single-mindedly ambitious, aggressive and ruthless; he was not a great general (the 1482 expedition to Scotland, on which his military reputation largely rests, was deliberately projected as a triumph by Gloucester himself, and the second Crowland continuator, for one, did not believe it) nor a chivalric hero; nor was he, by nature, a peacemaker or even a genuine man of the north. Until his brother Edward IV's death he pursued a career of continuous and conspicuous service to the Crown both on the national stage and in the north of England (where, increasingly, he came to see his future and where, certainly, he had achieved a notably dominant position by April 1483, albeit as a result of 'a judicious mixture of violence, chicanery and self-publicity'). His usurpation, the product of three months of calculated scheming and dissimulation (when he, first, systematically cut the ground from beneath his opponents' feet, and then, while the Yorkist establishment was still reeling, moved to press home his advantage by taking the throne itself), resulted not from principle or concern for the common weal but perceived personal advantage. Richard may have believed his own propaganda that he was indeed the man best suited to rule England, but it is doubtful if his behaviour aroused much enthusiasm in the political nation. During his early months as king he worked very hard, seemingly, to persuade people—especially his brother's former men—that his kingship was legitimate, projecting a notably positive image of himself as the very model of a just ruler. Buckingham's rebellion demonstrated the extent of his failure when virtually the whole Yorkist establishment in southern England, deeply hostile to his regime as it was, rose in arms against him. Moreover, although the king was able to contain the insurrection, many rebels fled abroad, many more only reluctantly made their peace (and remained dissatisfied), and, ominously, Henry Tudor had now emerged as a new focus for opposition. Richard III, forced to rely increasingly on his own personal affinity, exposed himself to charges of tyranny as a result; his enemies, in 1484–85, mounted a vigorous campaign of vilification against him; and his defeat and death at Bosworth appeared to justify all their vociferous criticisms.[35]

Hicks returned to the fray in 2003, not with a life of Richard but of Edward V, Richard's nephew. As Hicks himself says in his Preface when he was asked to write a biography of Edward V to fill a gap in the biographies of English kings he says that his first reaction was incredulity. Edward 'lived for only twelve years, reigned for only eleven weeks and then vanished. It could not be done'. On reflection Hicks decided that it could be done and he was quite right, it could be and he did it. Inevitably it is really a book about England in the lifetime of young Edward but as Hicks says while normally anything said about Edward is said in relation to the life of his father and his uncle viewing the events of Edward's life from his point of view gave a new perspective. As Hicks says 'approaching familiar scenes previously analysed and discussed in other books from this particular vantage point has compelled this biographer to plumb new sources, to recognise new insights, and to revise his interpretations' [chapter 1, p. 14]. This comment is borne out by the book and viewed from the perspective of the victim, his accession to the throne and deposition soon after do throw new light on the actions of Richard III and of how Richard would have viewed his nephew as a potential danger to his crown.

Following his *Edward V* Hicks wrote a life of Anne Neville, wife of Richard III. This is not as successful as Edward V. It is well written as expected with this author, but Anne played little part in the life of her husband, information about her is scanty. She played no obvious part in Richard's accession to the throne and a discussion of her life adds little to our knowledge of the life of her husband.[36]

A. J. Pollard, a seasoned campaigner in the Ricardian wars, published his perceptive, entertaining and superbly illustrated *Richard III and the Princes in the Tower* at about the same time as Michael Hicks's *Richard III: the Man Behind the Myth*. The inner man, Pollard concluded, must remain as enigmatic and elusive as ever. Even if, outwardly, Richard appears able, intelligent, self-confident (at any rate until the last months of his life), brave, chivalrous, generous, just and pious, there is no less a body of evidence showing him as a ruthless master of political intrigue and chicanery where his own personal ambitions and objectives were concerned. Until 1483 he was unswervingly loyal to Edward IV and, during the 1470s, he became both a great national figure and a powerful northern lord: indeed, in the north of England, he put an end to the civil strife that had plagued the region since 1453, actively promoted impartial justice and, by his victorious (and, among northerners, popular) campaign against the Scots in 1482, earned himself a formidable military reputation. Although there are no reliable indications that Richard entertained regal ambitions before 1483 and, even thereafter, it is not clear just when he set his sights on the throne, he certainly never surrendered the initiative once he had seized Edward V at Stony Stratford on 30 April: indeed, he very much dictated events, acted with a decisiveness and ruthlessness that completely wrong-footed his rivals, and made himself king at the end of June 1483 to the amazement of contemporaries and stunned paralysis of the Yorkist establishment. Yet his political judgement in taking the throne, an act that, in the end, led to his destruction rather than his preservation, is questionable; so, too, is the elimination of his nephews (whose murder he probably ordered before mid-September 1483), since rumours of their fate outraged many of his subjects and, no doubt, helped make them even less willing to accept him as king. Moreover, although largely restricted to southern counties from Essex to Cornwall (the north and midlands stood by the king) and poorly coordinated, Buckingham's rebellion *was* a serious affair. In its aftermath Richard certainly needed to destroy the makeshift alliance of Edwardian Yorkists and diehard Lancastrians who had backed it, secure the dissident south and eliminate the Tudor threat. Even the limited success of his early efforts, however, had a hollow ring to it and, as time passed, the king found himself having to rely ever more overtly on those whom he believed he could best trust (particularly members of his northern affinity); his credibility problem remained obstinately resistant to enduring solution; and, as the self-confidence he had exuded in 1483 evaporated, he may well have begun to crack under the strain during his last months. Finally, in August 1485, his own reckless behaviour in the field at Bosworth (a battle he should have won since he outnumbered his enemies and probably had the advantage of the terrain) brought not only his own death but also the downfall of the Yorkist dynasty.[37]

In 1993 much recent and new research found expression in an excellent collection of essays edited by John Gillingham: *Richard III: A Medieval Kingship*. Michael Hicks, for instance, reiterated and reinforced his argument that Richard of Gloucester was both a 'complex and many-sided man' and a 'formidable egotist'; Colin Richmond emphasized the obscurity of Richard's motives for usurping the throne, while also demonstrating that his decision to depose Edward V, once taken, proved disastrous for the Yorkist regime and dynasty; Rosemary Horrox made a powerful case for Richard III's seeing himself as 'the torch-bearer for Yorkist government', postulating that, if he had won the battle of Bosworth, 'he would probably have succeeded in building on his brother's achievements'; Anne Sutton demonstrated that, although the king's cultural tastes were nothing if not conventional, he had a clear conception of the non-political pursuits fitting for a king and what should be the proper role of the royal court; Michael K. Jones focused on Richard III as a courageous soldier, suggesting, moreover, that the military code at the heart of the king's self-image helps make sense of his political objectives and career; Alexander Grant argued powerfully, if controversially, that Bosworth, the eventual outcome of Richard's foreign policy, was 'not so much a Wars of the Roses battle as the final battle of the Hundred Years War'; and, in a lively historiographical survey, P. W. Hammond showed (not least in his strictures on James Gairdner's biography of the king) that Richard III certainly does not lack sympathizers even among the present generation of historians.[38]

Following this collection of essays the next major work on Richard III was another collection of published in 2001. This book, *The Worlds of Richard III*, consisted of valuable essays on the king by Professor A. J. Pollard, collected from a number of sources and written over the period from 1977 until 1992. Pollard explains in his introduction that these essays could be seen as preliminary and supplementary sketches to his two books *North Eastern England during the Wars of the Roses* and *Richard III and the Princes in the Tower*, published in 1990 and 1991. This is undoubtedly true but they stand very much on their merits as valuable discussions of various aspects of the life and career of Richard of Gloucester and his place in the history of north eastern England in his time. The essays start with three dealing with the development of the perception of the tyranny of Richard III and of whether or not he tyrannised the south by plantation of his northern supporters, and of a north south divide in English history, themes developed by Professor Pollard. Other essays deal with individuals and communities in the north east of England and their involvement with Richard, all bringing out aspects of an important part of Richard's life.[39]

Since this book was published there have been several biographies of Richard III but none of them major works. With the current rise of interest in the king we may perhaps expect that one is being written at this moment.[40]

NOTES

1. Recent discussions of the sources for Richard III, and his fascinating historiography, can be found in: Alison Hanham, *Richard III and his Early Historians 1483–1535* (Oxford, 1975); Charles Ross, *Richard III* (London, 1981); Antonia Gransden, *Historical Writing in England II c.1307 to the Early Sixteenth Century* (New York, 1982); Jeremy Potter, *Good King Richard?* (London, 1983); A. J. Pollard, *Richard III and the Princes in the Tower* (Stroud, 1991); Keith Dockray, *Richard III* (Headstart History pamphlet, Bangor, 1992); P. W. Hammond, 'The Reputation of Richard III', in *Richard III: A Medieval Kingship*, ed. John Gillingham (London, 1993). See also M. A. Hicks, 'The Sources', in *The Wars of the Roses*, ed. A. J. Pollard (London, 1995).

2. *Calendar of Patent Rolls, Edward IV, 1467–77, Edward IV–Edward V–Richard III, 1476–1485* (1899, 1901).

3. *British Library Harleian Manuscript 433*, ed. R. Horrox and P. W. Hammond, 4 vols (Richard III Society, 1979–83).

4. *Rotuli Parliamentorum*, ed. J. Strachey and others, 6 vols (1767–77), Vol. VI.

5. *York Civic Records*, Vol. I, ed. A. Raine (Yorkshire Archaeological Society Record Series, 1939). See also *York House Books*, ed. L. Attreed, 2 vols (Gloucester, 1991).

6. *Paston Letters 1422–1509*, ed. J. Gairdner, 6 vols (1904, reprinted Gloucester, in one volume, 1983). See also *Paston Letters and Papers of the Fifteenth Century*, ed. N. Davis, 2 vols (Oxford 1971–6).

7. *Stonor Letters and Papers 1290–1483*, ed. C. L. Kingsford, 2 vols (Camden Society, 1919).

8. *Plumpton Correspondence*, ed. T. Stapleton (Camden Society, 1839, reprinted Gloucester, 1990, with a new introduction by K. Dockray). See also *The Plumpton Letters and Papers*, ed. Joan Kirby (Camden Society, 1996).

9. Dominic Mancini, *The Usurpation of Richard III*, ed. and transl. C. A. J. Armstrong (Oxford 1969, reprinted Gloucester, 1984), especially pp. 57, 105. See also A. J. Pollard, 'Dominic Mancini's Narrative of the Events of 1483', *Nottingham Medieval Studies*, XXXVIII (1994).

10. *Crowland Chronicle Continuations 1459–1486*, ed. N. Pronay and J. Cox (Gloucester, 1986), especially pp. 95, 131, 181, 183, 193, and Pronay's introduction.

11. John Rous, *The Rous Roll* (1859, reprinted Gloucester, 1980), especially cap. 63, and *History of the Kings of England*, in A. Hanham, *Richard III and his Early Historians*, pp. 118–24.

12. Philippe de Commynes, *Memoirs: The Reign of Louis XI 1461–83*, transl. M. Jones (London, 1972), especially p. 355.

13. *Chronicles of London*, ed. C. L. Kingsford (1905, reprinted Gloucester, 1977), for *Vitellius AXVI* Robert Fabyan, *The New Chronicles of England and of France*, ed. H. Ellis (London, 1811); The Great Chronicle of London, ed. A. H. Thomas and I. D. Thornley (1938, reprinted Gloucester, 1983), especially p. 238.

14. Polydore Vergil, *Three Books of Polydore Vergil's English History*, ed. H. Ellis (Camden Society, 1844), especially pp. 173, 174, 180, 183, 187.

15. Sir Thomas More, *The History of King Richard III*, ed. R. S. Sylvester (Complete Works, Yale edn, 11, 1963). A new edition of the English version of More's *History*. The spelling and punctuation are modernized. There is an introduction and notes explaining the historical context.

16. Edward Hall, *The Union of the Two Noble Families of Lancaster and York* (1550, reprinted Scolar Press, 1970), 'King Richard III', especially f. 35.

17. William Shakespeare, *3 Henry VI* and *Richard III*. See also K. Dockray, 'William Shakespeare, the Wars of the Roses and Richard III', *History Teaching Review Year Book (Journal of the Scottish Association of Teachers of History)*, 11 (1997).

18. Sir George Buck, *The History of King Richard III*, ed. A. N. Kincaid (Gloucester, 1982), especially p. 208.

19. Horace Walpole, *Historic Doubts on the Life and Reign of Richard III*, ed. P. W. Hammond (Gloucester, 1987), especially pp. 121-3, 223.

20. Sharon Turner, *The History of England during the Middle Ages*, 3 vols (London, 1823).

21. Caroline Halsted, *Richard III as Duke of Gloucester and King of England*, 2 vols (1844, reprinted Gloucester, 1977), especially Vol. 2 pp. 485, 502-4.

22. J. R. Green, *A Short History of the English People* (London, 1874).

23. William Stubbs, *The Constitutional History of England*, Vol. 3 (Oxford, 1878), especially pp. 231-2.

24. James Gairdner, *History of the Life and Reign of Richard the Third* (2nd edn, Cambridge, 1898), especially pp. xi, 1.

25. Sir Clements Markham, *Richard III: His Life and Character* (London 1906, reprinted Bath, 1973), especially pp. 159-64, 282.

26. Philip Lindsay, *King Richard III* (London, 1933).

27. A. R. Myers, 'The Character of Richard III', *History Today*, iv (1954), reprinted in *English Society and Government in the Fifteenth Century*, ed. C. M. D. Crowder (London, 1967).

28. Paul Murray Kendall, *Richard the Third* (London, 1955), especially pp. 319, 323.

29. A. L. Rowse, *Bosworth Field and the Wars of the Roses* (London, 1966).

30. Charles Ross, *Richard III* (London, 1981).

31. Desmond Seward, *Richard III: England's Black Legend* (London, 1983), especially pp. 13, 15, 21.

32. Colin Richmond, '1485 and All That, or what was going on at the Battle of Bosworth?', in *Richard III: Loyalty, Lordship and Law*, ed. P. W. Hammond (London, 1986), especially p. 183.

33. Charles T. Wood, *Joan of Arc and Richard III* (Oxford, 1988), ch. 8 'The Deposition of Edward V' and ch. 9 'Richard III', especially pp. 170, 206. See also C. T. Wood, 'The Deposition of Edward V', *Traditio*, xxxi (1975).

34. Rosemary Horrox, *Richard III: A Study of Service* (Cambridge, 1989).

35. Michael Hicks, *Richard III: The Man Behind the Myth* (London, 1991), a revised edition was published as *Richard III* (Stroud, 2002. See also M. Hicks, *False, Fleeting, Perjur'd Clarence* (Gloucester, 1980) and *Richard III as Duke of Gloucester: A Study in Character* (Borthwick Paper, York, 1986).

36. Michael Hicks, *Edward V: the Prince in the Tower* (Stroud, 2003).

37. A. J. Pollard, *Richard III and the Princes in the Tower* (Stroud, 1991). See also A. J. Pollard *North Eastern England during the Wars of the Roses* (Oxford, 1990) and note 39 below.

38. *Richard III: A Medieval Kingship*, ed. John Gillingham (London, 1993): John Gillingham, 'Introduction: Interpreting Richard III'; Michael Hicks, 'Richard Duke of Gloucester: The Formative Years'; Colin Richmond, '1483: The Year of Decision (or Taking the Throne)'; Rosemary Horrox, 'The Government of Richard III'; Anne F. Sutton, 'The Court and its Culture in the Reign of Richard III'; Michael K. Jones, 'Richard III as a Soldier'; Alexander Grant, 'Foreign Affairs under Richard III'; P. W. Hammond, 'The Reputation of Richard III'.

39. A. J. Pollard, *The Worlds of Richard III*, (Stroud), 2001.

40. See Sean Cunningham, *Richard III: a Royal Enigma* (National Archives, 2003), this is a splendidly illustrated book; Josephine Wilkinson, *Richard III: the Young King to be* (Stroud, 2008); David Hipshon, *Richard III* (Abingdon, 2010). As well as these books two more were published covering Richard's reign. one only the last five months (John Ashdown-Hill, *The Last days of Richard III*, Stroud, 2010) and the other the full reign, (Peter Hammond, *Richard III and the Bosworth Campaign*, Barnsley, 2010).

RICHARD III: THE MAN AND THE KING

Many medieval English kings have bequeathed marvellous myths. Yet Richard III, arguably, has more claim to mythological distinction than any of them, since he has bequeathed not one enduring myth but two—as both an evil, murdering tyrant *and* an able, popular ruler.

An evil, murdering tyrant?

The first myth about Richard III—portraying him as a scheming, ruthless tyrant—not only developed early but also enjoyed the immense boost of receiving the blessing of England's greatest playwright, William Shakespeare. In its fullest flowering, this has it that Richard Duke of Gloucester (physically deformed and mentally warped as he was) set his sights on the throne as a very young man; he eliminated (or connived at the elimination of) Henry VI, Henry VI's only son Prince Edward of Lancaster, and even his own brother George Duke of Clarence, as a means of clearing the pathway to his own ambitions; and, once Edward IV was no more, he put his plans into action with a vengeance, cutting out the Woodvilles (the newly widowed Queen Elizabeth and her family), seizing his nephews Edward V and Richard Duke of York (and, in due course, securing their murder in the Tower of London), rigging the execution of William Lord Hastings (the man most likely to stand in his way), and, within less than three months, acquiring the crown for himself As king, he was unpopular from the start and, once the inevitably tyrannical nature of his rule fully revealed itself, he aroused such deep hostility and loathing in his oppressed people that they welcomed Henry Tudor Earl of Richmond with open arms: Richard's own death at Bosworth and Henry VII's triumphant accession, indeed, provided an only too fitting dénouement.

Even the king's contemporaries were frequently critical, most notably Dominic Mancini in his study of *The Usurpation of Richard III* (1) and the anonymous second continuator of the *Crowland Chronicle* (8). Regrettably, however, Mancini does not provide a detailed pen-portrait of Richard III (whereas he does include a lively character sketch of Edward IV); nor does the Crowland chronicler develop his hostile comments on the king's character and behaviour into a full-scale critique and assessment. John Rous, by contrast, could hardly contain his venom against Richard when writing his *History of the Kings of England* (9b); Philippe de Commines waxed lyrical on the king's intolerable pride and calculating cruelty (10); and the author of the *Great Chronicle of London* deeply disapproved of his behaviour as well (11). Polydore Vergil (12), Sir Thomas More (13) and Edward Hall (14) soon afterwards fashioned what they had learned of the last Yorkist into ever more compelling portraits of villainy: the myth of the evil, murdering tyrant now only awaited Shakespeare's dramatic genius to ensure its immortality.

An able, popular ruler?

The second myth about Richard III—suggesting that, but for his tragic death at Bosworth in August 1485, he might well have gone down in history as a most accomplished and successful king—can also be traced back to contemporary sources. Such a portrayal has it that, as Duke of Gloucester, Richard had been a loyal servant of his brother, an able ruler of the north and a successful soldier. His seizure of the throne, although dramatic and unexpected, was nevertheless justified in that it saved England from the horrors of a Woodville-dominated regime and preserved Richard himself from being unjustly humiliated. And, although he ruled for just two years, the quality of his government—particularly his zeal for impartial justice and concern for the well-being of ordinary folk—was only too apparent.

To some extent such a favourable image resulted from the king's own propaganda. The 1484 statute settling the crown on Richard III and his descendants, for instance, incorporated what purported to be a petition presented to him in June 1483, delivering a blistering attack on his brother Edward IV's regime and urging him to take the throne as a man of exemplary character devoted to good government and 'naturally inclined to the prosperity and common weal' of the realm (2). Nor can Thomas Langton Bishop of St David's be regarded as impartial; a northerner from Appleby in Westmorland, he was appointed to the bishopric of St David's during Richard's protectorate (in May 1483) and, in February 1485, rewarded with Lionel Woodville's former and much richer see of Salisbury. Yet it is surely significant that, when writing *privately* to his fellow humanist William Selling Prior of Christ Church, Canterbury, in September 1483, he highlighted the king's concern for justice and, especially, the welfare of his poorer subjects. John Rous, in the *Rous Roll* drawn up during Richard III's lifetime, similarly praised the king's good lordship and, in particular, his punishment of 'extortioners and oppressors of his commons' (9a). The Italian humanist Pietro Carmeliano who, after he had entered the service of Henry VII, was to pen a vituperative attack on the 'murderous tyrant' Richard III, portrayed him, in 1484, as a veritable paragon of virtue (3); while a Scottish envoy Archibald Whitelaw, in an oration to Richard during an audience in September 1484, flattered the king in even more extravagant terms (4). And, when news of Bosworth reached the city, it was put on record in York that Richard had been 'piteously slain and murdered, to the great heaviness of this city'. Indeed, even hostile Tudor commentators have the occasional word of commendation, among them Polydore Vergil who remarked that Richard's courage 'high and fierce... failed him not in the very death' when 'he rather yielded to be taken with the sword than by foul flight prolong his life'.

Neither monster nor mogul?

Richard III's personality remains as enigmatic as ever and his behaviour open to more than one interpretation. Evidently his reputation has indeed suffered at the hands of critical southern-orientated (especially London) chroniclers both before and after 1485 and, even more, evolving Tudor tradition during the sixteenth century: it is certainly unfortunate that there exists no contemporary or near-contemporary northern chronicle since, if there did, it might well have presented a very different perspective on the king. Nevertheless, historians must do the best they can with what evidence is available.

At least now we do have some factual evidence on Richard the man. The deformed Tudor monster still has to be rejected and, in particular Shakespeare's 'bottled spider' has no justification in reality. The skeleton excavated from the Greyfriars Friary in Leicester in September 2012 and identified as that of Richard III did however have a curved spine. This fairly severe scoliosis probably developed when Richard was a teenager; moreover, while it might well have been hardly noticeable in life it would have been seen only too clearly when he was carried naked to Leicester after his death. The skeleton showed that Richard's height was naturally about five feet eight inches, but this would have seemed significantly less when he was alive and so could justify the declaration of Scottish envoy William Whitelaw in 1484, that never had so much spirit and valour reigned in so small a body. Nicholas von Poppelau, a Bohemian knight who met the king in May 1484, reported that Richard was 'three fingers taller than myself, also much slimmer', and had 'delicate arms and legs': this too fits nicely with skeletal evidence that Richard was of slender build. Neither Von Poppelau nor Whitelaw mention a deformity which they may not have noticed and early portraits (such as that owned by the Society of Antiquaries) do not show one either. Later portraits, that of the king in Windsor castle, for instance, painted some thirty years after Richard's death (although probably based on a more nearly contemporary likeness) owes its deformed shoulder only to later alteration (as X-ray examination has made clear). John Rous, another contemporary writer describes Richard as having unequal shoulders, the left lower than the right and the skeleton confirmed that this was probably the case. Interestingly too we have the intriguing report (in the records of the City of York) of an unseemly incident as early as May 1491, when William Burton of York, a drunken schoolmaster, declared that 'King Richard was a hypocrite, a crookback, (who) who was buried in a dyke like a dog'.

The complex and contradictory judgements of contemporaries, near contemporaries and historians on Richard III's character cannot, in the last analysis, be reconciled. Clearly, he did not share Edward IV's exuberant love of pleasure; there is some evidence that his marriage of convenience to Anne Neville was not, on that account, entirely barren of affection; and the death of his only legitimate son in 1484 does appear to have caused him real distress. Yet he did sire at least one, possibly two, bastards; Thomas Langton, when accompanying the king on his post coronation progress, reported that 'sensual pleasure holds sway to an increasing extent'; and the Crowland chronicler believed that, during Christmas festivities in 1484, 'far too much attention was given to dancing and gaiety'. Richard III was certainly possessed of a wardrobe and jewellery fit for a king, while his court and its ceremonial reflected the exalted rank of regality no less than that of Edward IV. Yet his vituperative denunciation of his brother's regime, his condemnation of the morals of his opponents, and his humiliation of Edward IV's former courtesan Mistress Shore (2, 13) leave a nasty taste in the mouth; moreover, it is difficult to avoid the conclusion, given his own amoral (if not immoral) behaviour on occasion, that there was a streak of hypocrisy in him—as, indeed, there was a capacity for self-deception and a tendency to swallow his own hyperbolical propaganda. Indeed, he may even have developed a guilty conscience before the end: the Crowland continuator, for instance, reported that, the night before Bosworth, 'a multitude of demons' tormented him 'in a terrible dream', while Sir Thomas More learned that he 'never had quiet of mind' following his 'abominable deed' in murdering his nephews (13).

As A. J. Pollard has remarked, we can surely observe in Richard III 'a personal, knowledgeable and sincere piety': yet it is no less evident that he also had some of the less endearing characteristics of an early modern Puritan or even a present-day born-again Christian. His personal piety is perhaps best reflected in the religious books he is known to have possessed and much has certainly been made of his *Book of Hours* and the prayer composed for the king which it contains (7). In the 1470s he appears to have been an enthusiastic promoter of

daily worship in his chapel at Middleham in Yorkshire, where he also founded
a religious college and obtained his brother's permission to establish another
at Barnard Castle in Durham (5). As king he advanced a number of learned
clergy; his knowledge of Latin (as well as English and French) is perhaps
indicated by the fact that he attended scholarly disputations at Oxford in July
1483; and he certainly seems to have had a considerable interest in liturgy and
religious music. Nicholas von Poppelau attended a mass at Pontefract in May
1484 (at which the king was present) where he was particularly impressed by
the magnificent music, while there is record in *Harleian Manuscript 433* of
a royal warrant 'to seize for the king all singing men and children as can be
found in all the palaces, cathedrals, colleges, chapels, houses of religion and all
other places except Windsor royal chapel'. Yet a streak of puritanism surely
pervades a letter Richard despatched to his bishops in March 1484 (6).

Richard III, both before and after he became king, certainly enjoyed
projecting himself as a man of action, particularly in military matters, a fact
recognized by commentators during his own lifetime: a contemporary ballad
refers to him as 'the Duke of Gloucester, that noble prince, young of age and
victorious in battle'; Pietro Carmeliano remarked on his 'prudence in fostering
peace and waging war'; and, in his flattering oration of September 1484,
Archibald Whitelaw praised his 'strength of arms' and 'embodiment of military
skill' (3, 4). As constable of England in the 1470s, an overtly chivalric post, he
took his responsibilities very seriously indeed, revelling in military ceremonial
and the work of royal heralds, as well as delighting in his own family's martial
reputation and playing a major role in his father's reburial at Fotheringhay
in 1476. A capable military commander (as he demonstrated during the
expedition to Scotland in 1482) and very much at home in the company of
soldiers, there seems little doubt either that he was personally courageous (as
his behaviour on the battlefields of Barnet, Tewkesbury and Bosworth shows).
As an administrator, too, he was not without ability (as his record both in
the north of England and, later, as king amply demonstrates). Moreover, he
possessed a real capacity to inspire loyalty, as best shown by the firm backing he
generally received from his powerful northern connection. Yet, equally clearly,
he was inordinately ambitious for power, ruthless in his pursuit of it (even if this
involved dissimulation and deception) and capable not only of contemplating
but also sanctioning the removal of men (or children!) who stood in his way.

1) Dominic Mancini
(*Mancini*, pp. 59, 61, 81, 83)

Men say that in [his] will [Edward IV] appointed as protector of his children
and realm his brother Richard Duke of Gloucester, who shortly after

suppressed Edward's children and then claimed the throne for himself... [It] seems that in claiming the throne Richard was motivated not only by ambition and lust for power, for he also proclaimed that he was harassed by the ignoble family of the queen and the insults of Edward's relatives by marriage ...

[Since, following Edward's death] there was current in the capital a sinister rumour that the duke had brought his nephew not under his care but into his power, so as to gain the crown for himself, [he sent letters declaring that he] had not confined his nephew [but] rather had rescued him and the realm from ruin.... The deed had been necessary for his own safety and to provide for that of the king and kingdom.... Thenceforward he sought in every way to procure the good will of the people: hoping that, if by their support he could be proclaimed the only ruler, he might subsequently possess himself of the sovereignty with ease even against their wishes. After these letters had been read aloud in the council chamber and to the populace, all praised the Duke of Gloucester for his dutifulness towards his nephews and for his intention to punish their enemies. Some, however, who understood his ambition and deceit, always suspected where his enterprises would lead...

2) Rolls of Parliament: Act settling the crown on Richard III and his descendants, 1484
(*Rotuli Parliamentorum*, Vol. VI, pp. 240-2)

... we consider how that in the time of the reign of King Edward IV lately deceased, the order of all politic rule was perverted, the laws of God and of God's church and also the laws of nature and of England, [wherein] every Englishman is inheritor, broken, subverted and held in contempt, against all reason and justice, so that this land was ruled by self-will and pleasure, fear and dread, all manner of equity and laws laid aside and despised, whereof ensued many inconveniences and mischiefs, as murders, extortions and oppressions, namely, of poor and impotent people, so that no man was sure of his life, land, livelihood, nor of his wife, daughter, nor servant, every good maiden and woman standing in dread to be ravished and defouled...

[When] such as [Edward IV] had the rule and governance of this land, delighting in adulation and flattery and led by sensuality and concupiscence, followed the counsel of persons insolent, vicious and of inordinate avarice, despising the counsel of good, virtuous and prudent persons, the prosperity of this land daily decreased, so that felicity was turned to misery, and prosperity into adversity, and the order of policy, and of the law of God and man, confounded.

3) Pietro Carmeliano, 1484
(Dockray, *Richard III*, p. 14)

If we look (for) religious devotion, what prince is there in our time who shows a more genuine piety? If for justice, who can we reckon above him throughout the world? If we look for prudence in fostering peace and waging war, who shall we judge his equal? If we look for truth of soul, for wisdom, for loftiness of mind united with modesty, who stands before our King Richard? What Christian Emperor or Prince can be compared with him in good works and munificence? To whom are theft, rebellion, pollution, adultery, manslaughter, usury, heresy and other abominable crimes more hateful than to him? Obviously, no one.

4) Archibald Whitelaw's Address to Richard III, 12 September 1484
(*The North of England in the Age of Richard III*, ed. A. J. Pollard, pp. 193-5)

Most serene Prince and King: of all the sovereigns whom I have known, you stand out as the greatest—in the renown of your nobility, in your sway over your people, in your strength of arms, and in the wealth of resources at your command... [Your] most celebrated reputation for the practice of every form of virtue [has] reached into every corner of the world; moreover, there is the excellent and outstanding humanity of your innate benevolence, your clemency, your liberality, your good faith, your supreme justice, and your incredible greatness of heart. Your wisdom is not just human, it is almost divine: for you make yourself not simply at ease with important individuals, but courteous to the common people too... [Now] I look for the first time upon your face; it is a countenance worthy of the highest power and kingliness, illuminated by moral and heroic virtue. Fitting for you are the words which the post Statius used of the noble prince of Thebes:

Never before has nature dared to encase in a smaller body such spirit and such strength

and again:

In his small body the greatest valour held sway.

For you are the embodiment of military skill, prowess, good fortune and authority—all qualities which Cicero, in his eulogy of Pompey, declares should be sought in the best military leader.... In you, however, most serene Prince, all the requirements of a glorious king and general come together.... Were Cicero still alive, his skills would scarcely suffice to describe your virtues fully or sing your praises to the skies...

5) Chancery Patent Rolls
(*CPR, 1476-85,* p. 67)

a) *21 February 1478:* licence for Richard of Gloucester to found a college at Barnard Castle, within the castle there, of a dean and twelve chaplains, ten clerks and six choristers and one clerk, to pray for Edward IV and Elizabeth, Richard of Gloucester and Anne his wife, and heirs, and the souls of the king's father Richard late Duke of York, and the king's brothers and sisters, to be called the college of the said duke at Barnard Castle.

b) *21 February 1478:* licence for Richard of Gloucester to found a college at Middleham... to be called the college of the said duke at Middleham.

6) Richard III to the bishops, 10 March 1484
(*Harleian MS 433,* Vol. 3, p. 139)

... our principal intent and fervent desire is to see virtue and cleanness of living to be advanced, increased and multiplied, and vices and all other things repugnant to virtue, provoking the high indignation and fearful displeasure of God to be repressed and annulled.... We therefore will and desire you [that] you will see within the authority of your jurisdiction all such persons as set apart virtue and promote the damnable execution of sin and vices to be reformed, repressed and punished...

7) Richard III's Book of Hours: Prayer composed for the king
(Hammond and Sutton, *Richard III: The Road to Bosworth Field,* pp. 192-3)

Lord Jesus Christ, son of the living God, deign to free me, thy servant King Richard, from every tribulation, sorrow and trouble in which I am placed and from all the plots of my enemies, [and] deign [to] bring to nothing the evil plans that they are making or wish to make against me... I ask you, most gentle Lord Jesus Christ, to keep me, thy servant King Richard, and defend me from all evil, from the devil and from all peril present, past and to come, and deliver me from all the tribulations, sorrows and troubles in which I am placed... Lord, hear me, in the name of your goodness for which I give and return you thanks, and for all those gifts and goods granted to me... I ask you, most gentle Lord Jesus Christ, to save me from all perils of body and soul by your love, and to deign always to deliver and help me, and after the journey of this life, to deign to bring me before you, the living and true God...

8) Crowland Chronicle
(*Crowland*, pp. 159, 181, 183)

On 13 June [1483]... on the authority of the protector, Lord Hastings was beheaded... Thomas Archbishop of York and John Bishop of Ely... were imprisoned in different castles in Wales. In this way, without justice or judgement, the three strongest supporters of the new King were removed and, with all the rest of his faithful men expecting something similar, these two dukes [Gloucester and Buckingham] did thereafter whatever they wanted...

From that day [16 June 1483] both these dukes showed their intentions not in private but openly. Armed men in frightening and unheard-of numbers were summoned from the North, Wales and other districts within their command and power, and, on the 26th day of the same month of June, Richard, the protector, claimed for himself the government of the kingdom with the name and title of king, and, on the same day, in the great hall of Westminster, he thrust himself into the marble chair...

9) John Rous

a) The Rous Roll
(*The Rous Roll*, cap. 63)

The most mighty Prince Richard... all avarice set aside ruled his subjects in his realm full commendably, punishing offenders of his laws, especially extortioners and oppressors of his commons, and cherishing those that were virtuous, by the which discreet guiding he got great thanks of God and love of all his subjects, rich and poor, and great praise of the people of all other lands about him.

b) History of the Kings of England
(Hanham, *Richard III and his Early Historians*, pp. 120-1, 123)

Richard was born at Fotheringhay in Northamptonshire, retained within his mother's womb for two years and emerging with teeth and hair to his shoulders.... At his nativity Scorpio was in the ascendant.... And like a scorpion he combined a smooth front with a stinging tail. He received his lord King Edward V blandly, with embraces and kisses, and within about three months or a little more he killed him together with his brother. And Lady Anne, his queen, daughter of the Earl of Warwick, he poisoned.... And, what was the most detestable to God and all Englishmen, and indeed to all nations to whom it became known, he caused others to kill the holy man King Henry VI, or, as many think, did so by his own hands.... He was small of stature, with a short face and unequal shoulders, the right higher and the left lower...

This King Richard, who was excessively cruel in his days, reigned for three years and a little more, in the way that Antichrist is to reign. And like the Antichrist to come, he was confounded at his moment of greatest pride.

10) Philippe de Commines
(*Commines*, pp. 354-5)

The Duke [of Gloucester] had his two nephews murdered and made himself king, with the title King Richard. The two daughters [of Edward IV] were declared illegitimate in a plenary session of parliament and their right to the royal arms was taken from them. All his late brother's loyal servants, or at least those he could capture, were killed on his orders... [As] soon as King Richard had had his two nephews cruelly murdered, [he] lost his wife; some said he had her killed. He only had one son who died immediately afterwards.... This cruelty did not last long; for after he had become more filled with pride than any of his predecessors as kings of England in the last hundred years and he had killed the Duke of Buckingham and gathered a large army, God raised up an enemy [the Earl of Richmond] against him who had no power.... A battle was fought. King Richard was killed on the battlefield...

11) Great Chronicle of London
(*Great Chronicle*, p. 238)

And thus ended this man [Richard III] with dishonour as he that sought it, for had he continued still protector and suffered the children [of Edward IV] to have prospered according to his allegiance and fidelity, he should have been honourably praised over all, whereas now his fame is decried and dishonoured...

12) Polydore Vergil
(*Vergil*, pp. 226-7)

He reigned two years and so many months, and one day over. He was little of stature, deformed of body, the one shoulder being higher than the other, a short and sour countenance, which seemed to savour of mischief, and utter evidently craft and deceit. The while he was thinking of any matter, he did continually bite his nether lip, as though that cruel nature of his did so rage against itself in that little carcass. Also he was wont to be ever with his right hand pulling out of the sheath to the midst, and putting in again, the dagger which he did always wear. Truly, he had a sharp wit, provident and subtle, apt both to counterfeit and dissemble; his courage also high and fierce, which failed him not in the very death, which, when his men forsook him, he rather yielded to take with the sword than by foul flight to prolong his life...

13) Sir Thomas More
(*More*, pp. 7, 8, 54, 87)

Richard [was] in wit and courage equal with either of [his brothers], in body and prowess far under them both: little of stature, ill-featured of limbs, crook-backed, his left shoulder much higher than his right, hard-favoured of visage, and such as is in princes called warlike, in other men otherwise. He was malicious, wrathful, envious, and from afore his birth ever forward. It is for truth reported that the Duchess his mother had so much a do in her travail that she could not be delivered of him uncut, and that he came into the world with the feet forward... and, as the fame runs, also not untoothed.... No evil captain was he in war, to which his disposition was more suited than for peace. Sundry victories had he, and sometimes overthrows, but never for any lack in his own person, either of hardiness or generals hip. Free was he called of spending, and somewhat above his power liberal: with large gifts he got him unsteadfast friendship, for which he was fain to pillage and spoil in other places, and get him steadfast hatred. He was close and secret, a deep dissembler, lowly of countenance, arrogant of heart, outwardly companionable where he inwardly hated, not hesitating to kiss whom he thought to kill, pitiless and cruel, not for evil will always but oftener for ambition, and either for the surety or increase of his estate. Friend and foe were to him indifferent; where his advantage grew, he spared no man's death whose life withstood his purpose...

[The] protector sent into the house of Shore's wife [Jane or Elizabeth Shore, one of Edward IV's mistresses] and spoiled her of all that ever she had, about the value of two or three thousand marks, and sent her body to prison. And when he had a while laid unto her, for the manner's sake, that she went about to bewitch him, and that she was of council with the lord chamberlain [William Lord Hastings] to destroy him: in conclusion, when no plausibility could be fastened upon these matters, then he laid heinously to her charge the thing that she could not deny, that all the world knew was true, [that] she was free of her body. And for this cause—as a goodly continent prince, clean and faultless of himself, sent out of heaven into this vicious world for the amendment of men's manners—he caused the Bishop of London to put her to open penance, to go before the cross in procession upon Sunday with a taper in her hand…

[Following the murder of the Princes in the Tower] I have heard by credible report of such as were secret with his chamber-men that, after this abominable deed was done, he never had quiet in his mind, he never thought himself secure. Where he went abroad, his eyes whirled about, his body secretly armoured, his hand ever on his dagger, his countenance and manner like one always ready to strike back. He took ill rest at nights; lay long waking and musing, sore wearied with care and watch; rather dozed than slept, troubled with fearful dreams—suddenly sometimes start up, leap out of his bed and run about the chamber—so was his restless heart continually tossed and tumbled with the tedious impression and stormy   remembrance of his abominable deed.

14) Edward Hall
(Hall, *The Union of the Two Noble Families of Lancaster and York*, 'King Richard III', f. 35)

As he was small and little of stature, so was he of body greatly deformed, the one shoulder higher than the other, his face small, but his countenance was cruel, and such that a man at the first aspect would judge it to savour and smell of malice, fraud and deceit; when he stood musing he would bite and chew busily his nether lip, suggesting that his fierce nature in his cruel body always chafed, stirred and was ever unquiet; beside that, the dagger that he wore he would, when he studied, pluck up and down in the sheath to the middle, never drawing it fully out; his wit was pregnant, quick and ready, wily to fain and apt to dissimulate; he had a proud mind and an arrogant stomach…

RICHARD OF GLOUCESTER AND THE END OF THE HOUSE OF LANCASTER, c. 1469–71

Born at Fotheringhay in Northamptonshire in 1452, the youngest son of Richard Duke of York, Richard seems to have enjoyed a conventional aristocratic upbringing, becoming literate in English, French and probably Latin and, no doubt, proficient in the use of contemporary weaponry. Exiled for several months following the death of his father at the battle of Wakefield on 30 December 1460 (7), he returned to England in time to participate in his brother Edward IV's coronation on 28 June 1461 (when, despite his extreme youth, he was accorded the highest respect and deference) and, in the autumn of 1461, he was raised to the dukedom of Gloucester (2). By September 1465 he had been placed in the household of Warwick the Kingmaker and, although virtually nothing is known of his early teenage years, it is perhaps reasonable to assume that during the later 1460s he developed a considerable affection for Warwick's Yorkshire castle of Middleham and its surrounding countryside (which he retained for the rest of his life). Early in 1469 he was recalled to the royal court by Edward IV and, a few months later, created constable of England (at the age of seventeen) and given major responsibilities in Wales (1).

Certainly, during the crisis of 1469 to 1471 when Warwick challenged the Yorkist king's authority, he proved notably loyal to his brother: he fled to Burgundy with Edward in the autumn of 1470, shared his months in exile there, and returned with him to England in the spring of 1471 (3, 7, 10). When Edward sought entry into York on 18 March, Richard of Gloucester apparently commanded the small Yorkist force outside the city walls; he may well have helped facilitate the reconciliation between Edward and Clarence soon after (10); and, if we are to believe the *Great Chronicle of London*, he led the vanguard at the battle of Barnet on 14 April 1471 (8). The Burgundian chronicler Jean de Waurin certainly has him in the thick of the fighting, while a contemporary newsletter reported that he had been slightly wounded: at the very least he convincingly won his spurs during an extraordinary battle from which Edward IV eventually emerged victorious. At the battle of Tewkesbury on 4 May not only did Richard command the van but, according to the *Arrival*, played the key role in his brother's victory (3).

After Tewkesbury it was Richard of Gloucester, as constable of England, who presided over the trial and execution of a number of leading Lancastrians, while his alleged involvement in the murder of Prince Edward of Lancaster (Henry VI's son) following the battle was eventually to figure as the first major incident in later Tudor denigration of Richard III. In fact, the prince was almost certainly slain during the battle itself. Even if the official Yorkist account in the *Arrival* cannot be relied upon (3), the same cannot be said of the *Annals of Tewkesbury Abbey* (4) and *Warkworth's Chronicle* (2), both generally critical of the Yorkists, or Philippe de Commines (6) who probably obtained his information from Lancastrian exiles on the Continent. The Crowland continuator is non-committal (5), the London chronicles do not specifically name Gloucester (7, 8, 9), while even Polydore Vergil does not select him for special condemnation (10). There is a stronger case for Richard of Gloucester's involvement in the murder of Henry VI in the Tower of London soon after: the *Arrival*, implausibly, suggests he died 'of pure displeasure and melancholy' (3), and the Crowland chronicler is again very guarded (5), but Warkworth is less so (2), while both the London chronicles, Vergil and More report strong rumours of Gloucester's responsibility circulating in the early sixteenth century (7, 8, 9, 10, 11). Commines had few doubts but he is hardly to be relied on here (6). The balance of likelihood, indeed, is that Edward IV was responsible for Henry's death: Gloucester either played no part, in all probability, or merely acted in a supervisory capacity on his brother's behalf.

1) Chancery Patent Rolls
(*CPR, 1467-77*, pp. 178, 179, 180, 185)

a) *17 October 1469*: grant for life to the king's brother Richard Duke of Gloucester of the office of constable of England.

b) *7 November 1469*: appointment for life of Richard of Gloucester as chief justice of north Wales.

c) *30 November 1469*: appointment, during pleasure, of Richard of Gloucester as chief steward, approver and surveyor of the principality of Wales and the earldom of March in England, Wales and the Marches.

d) *7 February 1470*: appointment of Richard of Gloucester as chief justice of south Wales, the king's chamberlain in south Wales, and steward of lordships, manors etc. in south Wales.

2) John Warkworth's Chronicle
(*A Chronicle of the First Thirteen Years of the Reign of Edward IV*,
ed. J. O. Halliwell, pp. 1, 18, 21).

[At] the coronation of [Edward IV in 1461] he created and made dukes his
two brothers, the elder George Duke of Clarence, and his younger brother
Richard Duke of Gloucester...

And there was slain in the field [at Tewkesbury] Prince Edward, which cried
for succour to his brother-in-law the Duke of Clarence.... And the same night
that King Edward came to London, King Harry, being inward in prison in
the Tower of London, was put to death, the 21st day of May, on a Tuesday
night, between 11 and 12 of the clock, being then at the Tower the Duke of
Gloucester, and many others. And on the morrow he was chested and brought
to St Paul's, and his face was open that every man might see him...

3) Arrival of Edward IV
(*Historie of the Arrivall of Edward IV*, ed. J. Bruce, pp. 2, 3, 29, 30, 38)

The King [Edward IV] landed within Humber, on Holderness side, at a place
called Ravenspur [in March 1471].... The King's brother Richard, Duke of
Gloucester, and, in his company, 300 men, landed at another place four miles
from thence...

The King, full manly, set forth upon them [the Lancastrians at Tewkesbury]
and so also the King's vanguard, being in the rule of the Duke of
Gloucester...

In the winning of the field [at Tewkesbury] such as endured handstrokes
were slain at once. Edward, called Prince, was taken, fleeing towards the town,
and slain, in the field...

Here it is to be remembered that, from the time of Tewkesbury field, where
Edward, called Prince, was slain... in every part of England, where any
commotion was begun for King Henry's party, at once they were rebuked, so
that it appeared to every man... that the said party was extinct and repressed
for ever, without any hope of revival.... The certainty of all this came to the
knowledge of the said Henry, lately called King, being in the Tower of London
[and] he took it to such great hatred, anger and indignation that, of pure
displeasure and melancholy, he died the 23rd day of the month of May...

4) Annals of Tewkesbury Abbey

(*English Historical Documents* 1327–1485, ed. A. R. Myers, p. 314)

... on May 3rd [1471] ...there came to Tewkesbury Prince Edward, son of King Henry VI, with a great army.... When King Edward IV arrived with his army, he slew Prince Edward in the field...

These are the names of the noblemen that were slain at Tewkesbury field. Lord Edward, prince of King Henry, in the field of Gastum beside Tewkesbury, slain...

5) Crowland Chronicle

(*Crowland*, pp. 127, 129, 131)

... either on the battlefield [of Tewkesbury] or afterwards at the avenging hands of certain persons, there were killed Prince Edward, the only son of King Henry...

I shall say nothing, at this time, about the discovery of King Henry's lifeless body in the Tower of London; may God have mercy upon and give time for repentance to him, whoever it might be, who dared to lay sacrilegious hands on the Lord's Anointed! And so, let the doer merit the title of tyrant and the victim that of glorious martyr.

6) Philippe de Commines

(*Commines*, p. 196)

King Henry was a very ignorant and almost simple man and, unless I have been deceived, immediately after the battle [of Barnet] the Duke of Gloucester, Edward's brother, who after became King Richard, killed this good man with his own hand or at least had him killed in his presence in some obscure place...

[The] king was victorious [at Tewkesbury] and the prince of Wales was killed on the battlefield...

7) Vitellius AXVI

(*Vitellius AXVI*, pp. 174, 183, 184, 185)

[The] Duchess of York, hearing the loss of that field [second battle of St Albans, February 1461], sent over the sea her two young sons George and Richard, which went into Utrecht...

And during this parliament [in November 1470] King Edward [IV] was proclaimed through the city [of London] usurper of the crown, and the Duke of Gloucester his younger brother traitor, and both were attainted by the authority of the said parliament...

And in the beginning of April [1471] came King Edward with his brother the Duke of Gloucester [who landed] in the North country at a place called Ravenspur...

[At the battle of Barnet was King Edward IV], the Duke of Clarence, the Duke of Gloucester, the Lord Hastings with divers other lords...

And in May [1471] landed Queen Margaret and Prince Edward her son; and at Tewkesbury met with them King Edward, where was slain the said Prince Edward...

[King Henry] was slain, as it was said, by the Duke of Gloucester...

8) Great Chronicle of London
(*Great Chronicle*, pp. 216, 218, 220)

Upon the morn so soon as the day dawned, the captains enbattled their people upon either side [at Barnet], the Duke of Gloucester leading the vanguard of King Edward...

... after a short fight [at Tewkesbury] he [Edward IV] subdued his enemies and took Queen Margaret and her son alive. The which being brought unto his presence, after the king had questioned a few words of the cause of his so landing within his realm, and he gave unto the king an answer contrary to his pleasure, the king smote him on his face with the back of his gauntlet. After which stroke so by him received, the king's servants rid him out of life forthwith...

Upon Ascension Eve the corpse of King Henry VI was brought through Cornhill from the Tower with a great company of men of that place bearing weapons.... And so they conveyed him to St Paul's where that night he was set in the body of the church... open visaged that he might be known.... For him shortly afterwards God showed sundry miracles, of whose death the common fame then went that the Duke of Gloucester was not all guiltless.

9) Fabian's Chronicle
(*Fabian*, p. 662)

In the which battle [of Tewkesbury] she [Queen Margaret] was taken, and Sir Edward her son, and so brought unto the king. But after the king had questioned with the said Sir Edward, and he had answered him contrary to his pleasure, he then struck him with his gauntlet upon the face; after which stroke so by him received, he was by the king's servants at once slain upon the 4th day of the month of May...

Of the death of [Henry VI] diverse tales were told: but the most common fame went that he was stabbed with a dagger by the hands of the Duke of Gloucester which, after Edward IV, usurped the crown...

10) Polydore Vergil
(*Vergil*, pp. 133, 141, 152, 155–6)

[In the autumn of 1470 King Edward] went with his brother Duke of Gloucester unto [King's] Lynn, a town upon the sea coast, and, there finding a ship ready to make sail and pass the seas, he sailed into Flanders to Duke Charles... [When Edward IV and George Duke of Clarence in April 1471 came within view of one another, Richard Duke of Gloucester, as though he had been appointed arbiter of all controversy, first conferred secretly with the duke; then he returned to King Edward and did the very same with him. Finally, not war but peace was in every man's mouth; then, armour and weapons laid apart upon both sides, the brothers gladly embraced one another...

Edward the prince, an excellent youth, being brought a little after [the battle of Tewkesbury] to the speech of King Edward, and demanded how he dare be so bold as to enter and make war in his realm, made answer, with bold mind, that he came to recover his ancient inheritance; hereunto King Edward gave no answer, only thrusting the young man from him with his hand, whom forthwith, those that were present were George Duke of Clarence, Richard Duke of Gloucester and William Lord Hastings, cruelly murdered...

Henry the Sixth, being not long before deprived of his diadem, was put to death in the Tower of London. The continual report is that Richard Duke of Gloucester killed him with a sword, whereby his brother might be delivered from all fear of hostility. But whoever was the killer of that holy man, it is apparent enough that, as well the murderer and the procurers thereof, suffered punishment for their offences...

11) Sir Thomas More
(*More*, p. 8)

[Richard] slew with his own hands King Henry VI, being prisoner in the Tower, as men constantly say, and that without commandment or knowledge of the king, who would undoubtedly, if he had intended that thing, have appointed that butcherly office to some other than his own born brother.

3

RICHARD OF GLOUCESTER, CLARENCE AND THE COURT, C. 1471–83

During the crisis of 1469 to 1471 Richard of Gloucester's behaviour was in marked contrast to that of his elder brother George Duke of Clarence. In the later 1460s Clarence had fallen under the spell of Warwick the Kingmaker, married his elder daughter Isabel and backed the readeption of Henry VI in the autumn of 1470. No doubt dissatisfied at his treatment thereafter, he was reconciled with Edward IV (in April 1471) and, after Warwick's death at Barnet and Edward's restoration, clearly anticipated great rewards (not least from the Warwick inheritance). Gloucester, meanwhile, determined to marry the Kingmaker's younger daughter Anne himself, and the result of this, and the desire of both to reap maximum profit from royal patronage, was a great quarrel between the two brothers lasting well over two years, nicely recounted in the *Crowland Chronicle* (1) and commented upon in several of the *Paston Letters* (2). Gloucester did, in fact, marry Anne Neville; both he and Clarence benefited considerably from Edward's generosity; and the king eventually managed to engineer a reconciliation and settlement between his brothers, albeit at the expense of both Warwick's widow, the Dowager Countess Anne, and her six-year-old nephew George Neville (3). Within a few years, however, Clarence had been arrested and committed to the Tower (in July 1477), and, a few months after that, following a form of trial in parliament from which even the Crowland continuator's mind recoiled (1), he met a violent end, perhaps by drowning in a butt of malmsey wine (4, 6, 7, 8). Dominic Mancini, perhaps reflecting anti-Woodville propaganda disseminated by Richard of Gloucester in 1483, suggests that Queen Elizabeth Woodville engineered Clarence's fall, while Gloucester was overcome with grief at his brother's death (4). Later Tudor chroniclers concluded that Gloucester, already with an eye on the throne for himself, connived at Clarence's execution (or even perpetrated the deed himself): indeed, Sir Thomas More was already reporting strong rumours of this early in Henry VIII's reign (9). Certainly, it is interesting that the queen backed Gloucester against Clarence over the Warwick inheritance in the early 1470s; Gloucester, seemingly, attended the crucial planning meetings in late 1477 and helped pack the parliament that condemned his brother; and he benefited more than anyone else from Clarence's demise. John Rous, however, is non-committal on Clarence's fate (5), while Commines, the *Great Chronicle* and Vergil all place the responsibility for Clarence's death firmly on the shoulders of Edward IV (6, 7, 8). And, as the well-informed Crowland continuator makes clear (1), the king *himself* probably did play the pivotal role in bringing about Clarence's disgrace and destruction.

Richard of Gloucester's main role during the 1470s and early 1480s lay in the north of England: indeed, according to Dominic Mancini, following Clarence's death, anxious as he was to avoid the jealousy of the queen, he very rarely came to court (4). This does not, however, square with the known facts. As constable and admiral of England and, once Clarence was no more, great chamberlain as well (3f), he held national briefs; he possessed estates in southern as well as northern counties (3b); he attended parliamentary sessions in 1472-5, 1478 and 1483; he played a high profile role on ceremonial state occasions, such as the reburial of his father at Fotheringhay in 1476 and the wedding of his nephew Richard of York in 1478; and, since his name appears on every royal charter issued between February 1478 and January 1483, even in the last years of his brother's reign he clearly remained in close touch with both the court and central government. Certainly, too, in 1475 he provided the largest private contingent for Edward IV's invasion of France and, although Philippe de Commines reports his absence from peace negotiations and dissatisfaction with the treaty of Picquigny (6), he soon recognised it as a *fait accompli* and never wavered in his loyalty to the king.

1) Crowland Chronicle
(*Crowland*, pp. 131, 133, 145)

[The quarrel] in this Michaelmas term [1471] between the king's two brothers, and which proved difficult to settle, [began when] Richard Duke of Gloucester sought to make Anne [youngest daughter of the Earl of Warwick] his wife. This proposal did not suit the plans of his brother, the Duke of Clarence, married previously to the earl's elder daughter, who therefore had the girl hidden away so that his brother would not know where she was, since he feared a division of the inheritance. He wanted it to come to himself alone, by right of his wife, rather than to share it with someone else. The Duke of Gloucester, however, was so much the more astute that, having discovered the girl dressed as a kitchen-maid in London, he had her moved into sanctuary in St Martin's. As a result so much disputation arose between the brothers and so many keen arguments were put forward on either side with the greatest acuteness in the presence of the king, sitting in judgement in the council-chamber, that all who were present, even those learned in the law, marvelled at the profusion of the arguments which the princes produced for their own cases. These three brothers, moreover, the king and the dukes, possessed such outstanding talent that if they had been able to avoid dissension that triple cord could have been broken only with the utmost difficulty. Finally... King Edward, their loving brother, intervened and the whole dispute was settled: the Duke of Gloucester, once married to the aforesaid Anne, was to have such lands as were agreed between them, through arbitrators, with all that was left remaining in the possession of the Duke of Clarence; this left little or nothing at the disposal of the countess, the true lady and heiress of Warwick to whom, during her lifetime, the noble inheritance of Warwick and Despenser belonged...

The mind recoils from describing what followed in the parliament [of January 1478]—so sad was the dispute between two brothers [Edward IV and Clarence] of such noble character. No-one argued against the duke except the king; no-one answered the king except the duke...

[The] execution, whatever form it took, was carried out secretly in the Tower of London... in 1478. After this deed many people deserted King Edward who was now persuaded that he could rule as he pleased throughout the whole kingdom...

2) Paston Letters
(Paston Letters, Vol. 5, pp. 135-6, 188-9, 195, 199)

a) *Sir John Paston to John Paston, 17 February 1472*

... Yesterday the king, the queen, my lords of Clarence and Gloucester, went to Sheen to pardon; men say, not all in charity. What will fall, men cannot say...

The king entreats my lord of Clarence for my lord of Gloucester; and, as it is said, he answers that he may well have my lady his sister-in-law, but they shall part no livelihood, as he says. So what will fall I cannot say.

b) *Sir John Paston to John Paston, 3 June 1473*

... the Countess of Warwick is now out of Beverley sanctuary, and Sir James Tyrell conveys her northward, men say by the king's assent; whereto some men say that the Duke of Clarence is not agreed.

c) *Sir John Paston to John Paston, 22 November 1473*

... the world seems queasy here. For... it is said for certain that the Duke of Clarence makes him big in that he can, showing as he would but deal with the

Duke of Gloucester. But the king intends, eschewing all inconvenience, to be as big as both, and a stifler between them.

d) *Sir John Paston to John Paston, 22 November 1473*

… I trust to God that the two Dukes of Clarence and Gloucester shall be set at one by the award of the king.

3) Chancery Patent Rolls
(*CPR*, 1467-77, pp. 262, 297, 330, 344, 455, 1476–85, p. 67)

a) *18 May 1471*: grant for life to Richard Duke of Gloucester of the office of great chamberlain of England. Vacated by surrender and cancelled because the king granted the office to George Duke of Clarence, by other letters patent on 20 May 1472.

b) *4 December 1471*: grant to Richard Duke of Gloucester and the heirs male of his body of castles, honours, manors or lordships in Essex, Cambridge, Hertford, Suffolk, Kent, Buckingham, Oxford, Cornwall, Lincoln and Nottingham.

c) *18 March 1472*: George Duke of Clarence has surrendered a part of the grant of all castles, honours, lordships, manors and other possessions, late of Richard Earl of Warwick in his right or of Anne his wife, at the king's request, to his brother Richard Duke of Gloucester.

d) *20 May 1472*: grant for life to George Duke of Clarence of the office of great chamberlain of England, in lieu of a like grant of the office to the king's brother Richard Duke of Gloucester, by letters patent dated 18 May 1471, surrendered.

e) *6 June 1474:* confirmation, at the request of Richard Duke of Gloucester, of an act of Parliament to the effect that George Duke of Clarence and Isabel his wife, and Richard Duke of Gloucester and Anne his wife, daughters and heirs of Richard Neville late Earl of Warwick, and daughters and heirs apparent of Anne Countess of Warwick, should possess and enjoy, in the right of their wives, all possessions belonging to the countess as though she were naturally dead.

f) *21 February 1478*: grant for life to Richard Duke of Gloucester of the office of great chamberlain of England.

4) Dominic Mancini
(*Mancini*, pp. 63, 65)

... both [of Edward IV's brothers] were sorely displeased at the marriage [of the king to Elizabeth Woodville], yet one [who] was called Duke of Clarence vented his wrath more conspicuously, by his bitter and public denunciation of Elizabeth's obscure family.... But Richard [Duke] of Gloucester, being better at concealing his thoughts, [neither] did nor said anything that could be brought against him...

[The queen] concluded that her offspring by the king would never come to the throne unless the Duke of Clarence were removed; and of this she easily persuaded the king.... Accordingly, whether the charge was fabricated, or a real plot revealed, the Duke of Clarence was accused of conspiring the king's death by means of spells and magicians. When the charge had been considered before a court, he was condemned and put to death. The mode of execution preferred in this case was that he should die by being plunged into a jar of sweet wine. At that time Richard Duke of Gloucester was so overcome with grief for his brother that he could not dissimulate so well, but he was overhead to say that he would one day avenge his brother's death.

Thenceforth he came very rarely to court, [and] avoided the jealousy of the queen, from whom he lived far separated.

After the execution of the Duke of Clarence, and while Richard [kept] himself to his own lands, the queen ennobled many of her family. Besides, she attracted to her party many strangers and introduced them to court, so that they alone should manage the public and private business of the crown, surround the king, and have bands of retainers, give or sell offices, and finally rule the very king himself...

5) John Rous
(Hanham, *Richard III and his Early Historians 1483-1535*, p. 121)

And because there was a certain prophecy that after E.—that is, after Edward IV—G. should reign, for this ambiguity George Duke of Clarence, who was the middle brother between Edward and Richard, was killed on account of his name of George. And the other G., that is Gloucester, lived to fulfil the prophecy.

6) Philippe de Commines
(*Commines*, pp. 259, 89)

The Duke of Gloucester, the king of England's brother, and several others, who were not pleased at this peace [of Picquigny in 1475], were not present at this conference [between Edward IV and Louis XI of France]. But later they reconciled themselves to it and shortly afterwards the Duke of Gloucester came to visit the king [Louis XI] at Amiens and the king gave him some very fine presents, including plate and well-equipped horses...

King Edward had his brother, the Duke of Clarence, put to death in a pipe of malmsey because, it is said, he wanted to make himself king.

7) Great Chronicle of London
(*Great Chronicle*, p. 226)

... on the 18th day of February [1478] George, Duke of Clarence and brother to the king, who a certain time before had been held in the Tower as a prisoner, for considerations moving the king, [was] put secretly to death within the said Tower, and, as the fame ran, drowned in a barrel of malmsey.

8) Polydore Vergil
(*Vergil*, pp. 167-8)

[Edward IV] suddenly fell into a fact most horrible, commanding rashly and suddenly his brother George Duke of Clarence to be apprehended and put to death, who was drowned, as they say, in a butt of malmsey.... A report was even then spread amongst the common people that the king was afraid, by reason of a soothsayer's prophecy, and so became incensed against his brother George, which prophecy was that, after King Edward, should reign someone the first letter of whose name should be G... [Men] said afterwards that the same prophecy took effect when, after Edward, the Duke of Gloucester usurped the kingdom.... But it is very likely that King Edward right soon repented that deed; for, as men say, whensoever any sued to save a man's life, he was wont to cry out in a rage, 'O unfortunate brother, for whose life no man in this world would once make request'; affirming in that, manifestly, that he was cast away by envy of the nobility.

9) Sir Thomas More
(*More*, pp. 8-9)

Some wise men believe that [Richard of Gloucester's] drift, covertly conveyed, lacked not in helping forth his brother of Clarence to his death, which he resisted openly, howbeit somewhat, as men deemed, more faintly than he that were heartily minded to his welfare. And they that thus deem think that he long time in King Edward's life forethought to be king in case that the king his brother, whose life he looked that evil diet should shorten, should happen to decease, as indeed he did, while his children were young. And they deem that for this intent he was glad of his brother Clarence's death whose life must needs have hindered him so intending...

4

RICHARD OF GLOUCESTER, THE NORTH AND SCOTLAND, C. 1471–83

The Tudor chronicler Edward Hall believed that Richard III 'more loved, more esteemed and regarded the northern men than any subjects within his realm'; the second Crowland continuator, likewise, was of the firm opinion that Richard gave his greatest confidence to, and placed the greatest reliance on, men from the north of England; and historians, too, have been inclined to stress both the importance of Richard's northern background and connections by 1483 and the role of northerners during his protectorate and reign from 1483 to 1485. Probably first getting to know the north (especially Yorkshire) during his time in Warwick the Kingmaker's household in the later 1460s, Richard of Gloucester became a veritable northerner in his own right after 1471. Edward IV, in fact, chose to employ his brother as chief royal agent in the north in the 1470s and early 1480s, as warden of the west march against Scotland (1470), chief steward of the extensive Duchy of Lancaster estates in the north (1471), keeper of the forests beyond Trent and steward of Ripon (1472), sheriff of Cumberland (1475) and, finally, lieutenant-general of the north (1480). Gloucester's material advance in the north, both as a result of royal patronage and his vigorous personal efforts, is no less striking: most notably, he obtained Warwick the Kingmaker's former lordships of Middleham and Sheriff Hutton (Yorkshire) and Penrith (Cumberland) in 1471, Barnard Castle (Durham) and Scarborough (Yorkshire) in 1474, Skipton-in-Craven (Yorkshire) in 1475, and Richmond and Helmsley (Yorkshire) in 1478. Many of these acquisitions, both office and land, can be found registered on the *Patent Rolls* (1). There are nice indications in public records, as well, of his building a powerful northern retinue for himself, drawn not least from families (like the Conyers and Metcalfes in Richmondshire) formerly of Neville persuasions (2). Similarly, there is ample evidence of his growing role in northern government and administration.

Inevitably, the advancement of this royal parvenu was a matter of concern to the heads of well-established northern families like Henry Percy Earl of Northumberland, Ralph Neville Earl of Westmorland and Thomas Lord Stanley. Relations between Gloucester and Northumberland, in particular, were very uneasy in the early 1470s until, in July 1474, the two great lords sealed an agreement whereby Percy recognized Richard's overall predominance and the duke promised to be the earl's 'good and faithful lord at all times' (3). Thereafter, in practice, Richard of Gloucester accepted that Northumberland and the East Riding of Yorkshire were Percy spheres of influence, while the royal duke enjoyed a more or less free hand in most of the rest of Yorkshire and the north-west: the Percy earl's continued predominance in the West Riding honour of Knaresborough, however, is graphically highlighted in the *Plumpton Correspondence* (4a). Nevertheless, as A. J. Pollard has demonstrated in his definitive 1990 study of *North Eastern England during the Wars of the Roses*, during the 1470s Richard of Gloucester established a regional hegemony in the north eclipsing even that enjoyed by Warwick the Kingmaker in the 1460s: in the process he reunited north-eastern society, created a formidable personal following and brought a degree of stability to the region not seen for years.

Richard of Gloucester not only restored real peace and stability to the north after the upheavals of the 1450s and 1460s but also provided sound government and administration. Frequently working in tandem with Henry Percy Earl of Northumberland, he vigorously promoted the cause of impartial justice, whether by enforcing legislation more effectively than hitherto or arbitrating in private disputes (1j, 4a, 5a, c); his household council can evidently be regarded as a precursor of the Council of the North (formally established by Richard III in 1484); the city of York certainly recognized the value of the duke's good lordship and support (5b, f, g); and Dominic Mancini's informants, in 1483, clearly led *him* to believe that Richard had deliberately 'set out to acquire the loyalty of his people through favours and justice' during Edward IV's last years (9). Most critical of all, perhaps, was Richard of Gloucester's role in defending the Anglo-Scottish frontier zone and, in the early 1480s, waging war against Scotland.

Certainly, for the lords, gentry and, indeed, ordinary inhabitants of the northern (especially border) counties, relations with Scotland were of paramount importance and there is evidence of anxiety about the Scots even when the two kingdoms were at peace (1f). Throughout the 1470s Gloucester, as warden of the west marches, kept a close eye on his deputies, visited the border himself, and spent money on defence works (such as improvements to Carlisle castle). Towards the end of the decade, as Anglo-Scottish relations deteriorated, Scotland became an ever more pressing preoccupation. When the long-standing truce with James III of Scotland finally broke down, Edward IV appointed his brother, in May 1480, as king's lieutenant to resist the Scots and, in June, issued commissions (headed by Gloucester and Northumberland) to array men in the north for the purpose (1h, i, 6). Further measures to counter the Scottish threat by force, in September 1480, are reported in both the *Plumpton Correspondence* and the *York Civic Records* (4b, 5d, e). Richard of Gloucester, arguably, had long wished for a more aggressive stance against Scotland, and events in 1480 played into his hands: both Louis XI of France, according to the Crowland continuator, and James III's younger brother Alexander Duke of Albany had put pressure on the Scottish king to break the truce with England; Edward IV, probably urged on by *his* brother, had no choice but to respond; and borderers, on both sides of the Anglo-Scottish frontier, were enthusiastic for a renewal of war. In August 1481 Gloucester and Northumberland besieged Berwick but a Scottish counter-attack on Percy territories forced them to withdraw. Then, in July 1482, a major expedition into Scotland was mounted, nominally in support of Albany's claim to the Scottish throne, Albany having promised to accept English overlordship and surrender much of south-western Scotland if the venture proved successful. Again, Edward IV had probably sanctioned the campaign at his brother's urging and, certainly, Gloucester (accompanied by Henry Percy Earl of Northumberland, Thomas Lord Stanley and many other prominent northerners) had at his disposal one of the largest English armies raised in the fifteenth century (about 20,000 men). Unfortunately, the expedition only had financing for a single month and, although Gloucester's forces reached Edinburgh, the incarceration of James III by a group of his own nobility (preventing his fighting the full-scale battle Richard was probably hoping for) and Albany's failure to honour his side of the bargain, soon compelled the English to abandon a probably futile siege of Edinburgh castle and withdraw. A detachment of the army did, however, succeed in seizing the border town of Berwick (7, 10, 11). The Crowland chronicler is notably scathing about the expedition and its outcome (10), but Edward IV himself seems to have been satisfied enough (7) and, from Gloucester's (and the borderers') standpoint, it had been a daring and spectacular campaign (not least since Berwick's capture significantly strengthened the defences of north-eastern England). Perhaps Gloucester's real ambitions lay in south-western Scotland, however, where he hoped to carve out a principality for himself; if so, the notably generous royal grant of January 1483 must have pleased him no end since not only did he become hereditary warden of the west marches and a virtual viceroy in Cumberland but he also received sanction to hold as a palatinate any lands he might conquer across the western border in Scotland (8).

1) Chancery Patent Rolls

(*CPR*, 1467–77, pp. 260, 338, 408, 485, 549, 1476–85, pp. 50, 90, 205, 213-14, 339)

a) *29 June 1471*: grant to Richard of Gloucester and heirs male of the castles, manors and lordships of Middleham and Sheriff Hutton, co. York, and Penrith, co. Cumberland.

b) *18 May 1472*: grant for life to Richard of Gloucester of the office of keeper of the forests beyond Trent.

c) *10 September 1473*: commission to Richard of Gloucester to array the king's lieges of the county of York and bring them to the king's presence with all speed when required.

d) *18 February 1475*: appointment of Richard of Gloucester as sheriff of Cumberland for life.

e) *12 June 1475*: grant to Richard of Gloucester and the heirs of his body of the honour, castle, manor and lordship of Skipton-in-Craven, lately belonging to John late Lord Clifford, attainted.

f) *18 June 1477*: commission to Richard of Gloucester, and others, to enquire into the report that diverse Scots, women as well as men, wander about various parts of the county of York, especially the West Riding, and have burnt diverse houses and buildings; and to arrest and imprison the offenders and their instigators. The like to Henry Earl of Northumberland, and others, in the East Riding.

g) *5 March 1478*: grant to Richard of Gloucester and the heirs of his body of the castle of Richmond, and feefarm of the town of Richmond, in Yorkshire.

h) *12 May 1480*: appointment of Richard of Gloucester as king's lieutenant to fight against James, King of Scotland, who has violated the truce lately concluded with the king, and his adherents, with power to call out all the king's lieges in the marches towards Scotland and adjacent counties.

i) *20 June 1480*: commissions of array, headed by Richard of Gloucester and Henry Earl of Northumberland, issued for the three ridings of Yorkshire, Westmorland, Cumberland and Northumberland, for defence against certain men of Scotland who have burnt townships and dwellings in the marches and imprisoned and slain the king's lieges.

j) *25 February 1483*: commission to Richard of Gloucester, Henry Earl of Northumberland, and others, to enquire into discords between the king's tenants of the forest of Knaresborough on the one part and the tenants of Lady Berkeley and the abbot and convent of St. Mary, Fountains, and the other inhabitants of the free chase of Nidderdale, co. York, on the other part, concerning the bounds between the forest and the chase.

2) Northern Retainers of Warwick the Kingmaker and Richard of Gloucester: the Conyers and the Metcalfes

a) *Fee'dmen of Warwick*, 1465/6
(Public Record Office, SC6/1085/20)

Sir John Conyers, steward in Richmondshire, fee £13/6/8d
William Conyers Esquire, £2
Richard Conyers, receiver, £4
James Metcalfe Esquire, £3/6/8d
Brian Metcalfe Esquire, £2
Miles Metcalfe, attorney-general, £10
Alfred Metcalfe, forester, £3/0/8d
Richard Metcalfe, forester, £3/0/8d
Geoffrey Metcalfe, forester, £1/10/od
Alexander Metcalfe, forester, £1
Reginald Metcalfe, Edward Metcalfe and Thomas Shaw, £1/10/od

b) *Fee'dmen of Gloucester*, 1473/4
(Public Record Office, DL29/648/10485)

Sir John Conyers, steward in Richmondshire, £20
Sir Richard Conyers, £6/13/4d
John Conyers Esquire, £6/13/4d
William Conyers Esquire, bowbearer, £2
Richard Conyers, receiver of Middleham, £6/13/4d
Richard Conyers junior, £6/13/4d
Thomas Metcalfe Esquire, £6/13/4d
Brian Metcalfe Esquire, £2
Dionisius Metcalfe, reeve, 13/4d

3) Indenture between Richard Duke of Gloucester and Henry Percy Earl of Northumberland, 28 July 1474
(*England under the Yorkists*, ed. I. D. Thornley, pp. 147-8)

This indenture made the 28th July [1474] between the right high and mighty prince Richard Duke of Gloucester on the one part and the right worshipful lord Henry Earl of Northumberland on the other...

[The earl] promises and grants to the duke to be his faithful servant, the duke being his good and faithful lord. And the earl to do service unto the duke at all times lawful and convenient, when he by the duke shall be lawfully required, the duty of allegiance of the earl to the king's highness... first at all times reserved.

For which service the duke promises and grants to the earl to be his good and faithful lord at all times.... Also, the duke promises and grants to the earl that he shall not ask, challenge or claim any office or offices or fee that the earl has of the king's grant.... And also the duke shall not accept or retain into his service any servant or servants that were or are by the earl retained of fee, clothing or promise, according to the appointments taken between the duke and earl by the king's highness and the lords of his council at Nottingham 12th May [1473].

4) Plumpton Correspondence
(*Plumpton Correspondence*, pp. 31-3, 40)

a) *Godfrey Green to Sir William Plumpton, 8 November c. 1476*

... I have received from you diverse letters [requiring] that I should labour to Sir John Pilkington to labour to my lord of Gloucester or to the king; they to move my lord of Northumberland that you might occupy still at Knaresborough... [It] is thought here by such as love you that that labour should rather hurt in that matter than avail; for it is certain, as long as my lord of Northumberland's patent stands good, he will have no deputy but such as shall please him...

And as to another point contained in your writing, that is, to inform the lords and their counsel of the misgovernances of Gascoigne and his affinity, [by] your council [it] is thought here that it would be ... a disworship to my lord of Northumberland who has the chief rule there under the king...

And as for the message to my lord chamberlain, when I laboured to him that you might be justice of the peace, he answered thus—that it seemed by your labour and mine that we should make a jealousy between my lord of Northumberland and him... . Sir, I took that for a watchword for meddling between lords.

b) *Henry Earl of Northumberland to Robert Plumpton Esquire, 7 September 1480*

... the Scots in great number are entered into Northumberland, whose malice, with God's help, I intend to resist; therefore, on the king our sovereign lord's behalf, I charge you, and also on mine as warden [of the east and middle marches], that you, with all such persons as you may bring in their most defensible array, be with me at Topcliffe on Monday by 8 o'clock...

5) York Civic Records
(*York Civic Records*, Vol. 1, pp. 2-3, 15-16, 24, 34-5, 36, 51-2, 54, 60)

a) *13 March 1476*

The king our sovereign lord straitly charges and commands that no man, of whatever condition or degree, make, or cause to be made, any affray, or any other attempt, whereby the peace of the king should be broken.... And, over this, the right high and mighty prince, Richard Duke of Gloucester, great constable and admiral of England, and the right noble lord, Henry Earl of Northumberland, on the king's behalf, straitly charge and command that every man observe, keep and obey all the premises...

b) *31 December 1476*

... by the mayor and council it was wholly agreed and assented that the Duke of Gloucester shall, for his great labour... made to the king's good grace for the conservation of the liberties of this city, [be] presented at his coming to the city with six swans and six pikes...

c) *Richard of Gloucester to the city of York, 15 November 1477*

[According] to your desires [regarding] Goldale garth or any others, we have moved the king's grace on the matter and [he] has commanded us at our next meeting to take a view and oversight of such garths and weirs, and, [if they] have not been allowed before justices of eyre, see that they be pulled down; the which, or any other thing we may do for the welfare of your city, we shall put us in our utmost devoir and good will...

d) *Richard of Gloucester to the city of York, 8 September 1480*

... the Scots in great multitude intend this Saturday night to enter into [the] marches of these north parts.... We trusting to God to... resist their malice... desire and require you to send unto us at Durham, on Thursday next, a servant of yours accompanied with such certain number of your city defensibly arrayed, as you intend and may deserve right special thanks from the king's highness and us...

e) *Edward IV to the city of York, 19 October 1480*

... by the report of our dearest brother the Duke of Gloucester, we have understood to our full good pleasure your ready disposition to serve us in his company against our enemies and rebels the Scots, for which we tenderly thank you and pray for your continuance in the same; letting you know that, in such reasonable things as you shall have to do with us hereafter, we shall therefore so remember your dispositions as shall be to your welfare and honour in time to come.

f) *12 March 1482*

... it is agreed that for the great labour, good and benevolent lordship that the right high and mighty prince the Duke of Gloucester has at all times done for the welfare of this city, [he shall receive] praise and thanks...

g) *14 May 1482*

... the Duke of Gloucester [intends] to enter Scotland on Wednesday next [for] subduing the king's great enemy the king of Scots and his adherents. And, since the duke at all times has been a benevolent, good and gracious lord to this city, it was thought... speedful and also thankful... to send to him a certain people, well and defensible arrayed...

h) *15 August 1482*

... it was agreed that, since the soldiers of this city now with my lord of Gloucester in Scotland [are] desolate of money, a tax be raised of the parishes of this city for seven days' wages...

6) Royal Proclamation, 12 June 1482
(Hammond and Sutton, *Richard III: The Road to Bosworth Field*, p. 83)

James King of Scotland... decided to wage war... against us and invade our realm by sudden and armed attack. We therefore... trusting with full powers our illustrious brother, Richard Duke of Gloucester, in whom not only for his nearness and fidelity of relationship but for his proved skill in military matters and his other virtues, we name, depute and ordain him our Lieutenant General... to fight, overcome and expel the said King of Scotland, our chief enemy, and his subjects, adherents and allies, however great the fight may be...

7) Venetian State Papers, Edward IV to Pope Sixtus IV, 25 August 1482
(*Venetian State Papers, pp. 87-8*)

... the army which our brother lately led into Scotland, traversing the heart of that kingdom without hindrance, arrived at the royal city of Edinburgh, and found the king with the other chief lords of the kingdom shut up in a most strongly fortified castle, no wise thinking of arms, of resistance, but giving up that right fair and opulent city into the power of the English who... spared the supplicant and prostrate citizens.... The chief advantage of the whole expedition is the reconquest of the town and castle of Berwick...

8) Rolls of Parliament, January 1483
(*Rotuli Parliamentorum*, Vol. VI, pp. 204-6)

[The King, Lords and Commons] understand and consider that the Duke [of Gloucester], being Warden of the West Marches, by his diligent labours... has subdued a great part of the west borders of Scotland, adjoining England, by the space of thirty miles and more... and has [secured] divers parts thereof to be under the obedience of [the King] to the great surety and ease of the north parts of England, and much more thereof he intends and with God's grace is likely to get and subdue...

[The King grants] that the Duke shall have to him and his heirs male [the] Wardenship of the West Marches of England.... And also [the] making and ordaining of the sheriff of the county of Cumberland. And also... to him and his heirs in fee simple the countries and ground in Scotland [and] the West Marches [which] the Duke or his heirs have or shall hereafter... get and achieve. And the Duke and his heirs forever shall have as large power, authority, jurisdiction, liberty and franchise [there] as the Bishop of Durham has within the bishopric of Durham...

9) Dominic Mancini
(*Mancini*, pp. 63, 65)

[Following Clarence's death Richard of Gloucester] came very rarely to court. He kept himself within his own lands and set out to acquire the loyalty of his people through favours and justice. The good reputation of his private life and public activities powerfully attracted the esteem of strangers. Such was his renown in warfare that, whenever a difficult and dangerous policy had to be undertaken, it would be entrusted to his discretion and his generalship.

By these skills Richard acquired the favour of the people and avoided the jealousy of the queen, from whom he lived far separated.

10) Crowland Chronicle
(Crowland, pp. 147, 149)

... the Scots shamelessly broke the thirty years' truce we had made with them.... In consequence Edward proclaimed a terrible and destructive war against the Scots, with Richard Duke of Gloucester, the king's brother, in command of the whole army. What he achieved in this expedition and what large sums of money, repeatedly extorted under the name of benevolence, he foolishly used up were amply demonstrated by the outcome of the business. Thus, having got as far as Edinburgh with the whole army without meeting any resistance, he let that very wealthy town escape unharmed and returned through Berwick; the town there had been captured at the outset of the invasion and the castle, which held out longer, finally fell into English hands though not without slaughter and bloodshed. This trifling gain, or, perhaps more accurately, loss, for the maintenance of Berwick costs 10,000 marks a year, diminished the resources of the king and kingdom by more than £10,000 at the time. King Edward was grieved at the frivolous expenditure of so much money, although the recapture of Berwick alleviated his grief for a time. This is what the duke accomplished in Scotland during the summer of 1482...

11) Polydore Vergil
(Vergil, pp. 169-70)

[The] Scottish king... broke truce with England, and molested the borders thereof with sudden incursions; wherefore King Edward, with great indignation, determined to make war upon Scotland... [Therefore] he addressed forthwith against the Scots Richard his brother, Duke of Gloucester, Henry the fourth Earl of Northumberland, Thomas Stanley, and the Duke of Albany, with an army royal.... The Duke of Gloucester, entering Scotland, wasted and burned all over the country, and, marching further into the land, encamped himself not far from his enemies; when, perceiving that not one man of all the Scottish nation resorted to the Duke of Albany, he suspected treason, not without cause; wherefore he took truce with King James, and returned the right way to Berwick, which in the meantime Thomas Lord Stanley had won, without loss of many men.

5

THE POLITICAL LEGACY OF EDWARD IV, APRIL/MAY 1483

No one will ever know for certain whether Richard of Gloucester set his sights on the throne immediately he heard of Edward IV's sudden death on 9 April 1483, as suggested by early Tudor sources like Polydore Vergil and Sir Thomas More, or if, at first, he merely intended to secure control of his nephew Edward V so as to ensure a central role for himself in either a minority council or the new king's own government. What is tolerably certain is that, within weeks of Edward IV's death, such was his craving for security and power that all manner of rumours and suspicions became rife (thoroughly confusing contemporaries) until, eventually, he seized the Crown for himself and engineered his own coronation as Richard III on 6 July 1483. Even so, Edward IV cannot be entirely cleared of blame for what happened after his demise: his son and heir was only twelve years old and had long resided at Ludlow in a Woodville-dominated environment; the queen and her family, even if not as grasping and unpopular as probably Ricardian-inspired propaganda led Dominic Mancini to believe (1), clearly entertained well-founded expectations of a prominent position for themselves in the new regime; the dead king's only surviving brother (who, arguably, had the best claim to be protector should the council follow the precedent established by Henry V's equally unexpected death in 1422) was an immensely powerful and ambitious northern lord who (in part at least as a result of Edward IV's generous and sustained patronage) packed a good deal of political clout; and, although exaggerated by Mancini and More (1, 5), there were divisions in the royal court (most notably between the late king's closest and most loyal supporter William Lord Hastings and the queen's son Thomas Grey Marquis of Dorset). Certainly, too, there is evidence that Gloucester believed himself to be vulnerable in the political climate occasioned by his brother's premature death, not least on account of his insecure title to so many of his estates: his precarious hold on the northern Neville lands, in particular, may have provided him with a powerful motive for decisive action (a fact graphically brought home to him by the death of George Neville on 4 May 1483, since his right to much of his northern property was now reduced to a mere life interest). Yet it is Gloucester's *behaviour*, whatever his motivations, that dominated the action-packed months April to July 1483.

Even if, as seems likely, the notion of a long-standing feud between Richard of Gloucester and the Woodvilles (1) is no more than the product of hastily concocted propaganda justifying the duke's moves against them, there is no doubt that a massive gulf *did* rapidly open up between Gloucester and the queen's family once Edward IV was no more. There seems little doubt either that, in April and May 1483, William Lord Hastings gave firm backing to Gloucester as the best means of establishing Edward V on the throne and securing his coronation (as he thought!): both Mancini and the Crowland continuator, our best-informed narrative sources, suggest that Hastings played a crucial role in advancing Gloucester's claims in April 1483 (not least since he had little time for either the queen or her family), while early Tudor writers were no less convinced of his commitment to ensuring the primacy of the royal duke during the young king's early months (1, 2, 4, 5). Richard of Gloucester, meanwhile, played his own cards with considerable skill, whether from genuine concern to outmanoeuvre the Woodvilles on behalf of his nephew or (more probably) flagrant dissimulation in his own self-interest: apparently, he despatched letters from the north of England to both queen and council declaring his loyalty to Edward V, presided over a commemoration service for his late brother in York and (in company with many northern nobility and gentry) swore a solemn oath of fealty to the new king, and then marched south with a large retinue, perhaps on the advice of Hastings who had already persuaded Elizabeth Woodville that her son need only bring a moderate escort to London (1, 2). On 29 April 1483 Gloucester, and his no doubt predominantly northern entourage, arrived at Northampton: there he joined forces with Henry Stafford Duke of Buckingham (who had his own reasons for disliking the Woodvilles and may, even, have helped poison Richard's mind against them), entertained the queen's brother Anthony Earl Rivers and her son Sir Richard Grey and, next morning, promptly arrested the pair of them (1, 2). Proceeding to nearby Stony Stratford, he took possession of his probably indignant royal nephew, arrested his companions (including Sir Thomas Vaughan) and sent them (along with Rivers and Grey) to the northern stronghold of Pontefract (1, 2, 3, 4). News of her brother-in-law's dramatic initiative soon reached Elizabeth Woodville in London and, no doubt thoroughly alarmed, she hastily took sanctuary in Westminster Abbey, along with her daughters and younger son Richard of York (1, 2, 4, 5). With rumour, suspicion and fear seemingly rife in the capital, Richard of Gloucester's real intentions probably now became the subject of increasing speculation (1, 2, 4). Nevertheless, once Gloucester, Buckingham and the young king entered London on 4 May (amid vigorous propaganda alleging pernicious Woodville conspiracy), a new date in late June was set for Edward V's coronation and, on 10 May, Gloucester was formally appointed protector of the realm by the council.

1) Dominic Mancini
(*Mancini*, pp. 59, 71, 73, 75, 79, 83)

Now Edward IV, who ruled England with great renown, died on 7 April in London...

At his death his brother Richard was living on the Gloucester estates, two hundred miles distant from the capital. Edward the king's son... was residing in the province of Wales.... The queen with her second son, the Duke of York, and the rest of her family were in London.... The royal treasure... was kept in the hands of the queen and her people... [The] problem of the government during the royal minority was referred to the consideration of the barons. Two opinions were propounded. One was that the Duke of Gloucester should govern, because Edward in his will had so directed, and because by law the government ought to devolve on him. But this was the losing resolution; the winning was that the government should be carried on by many persons among whom the duke, far from being excluded, should be accounted the chief.... All who favoured the queen's family voted for this proposal, as they were afraid that, if Richard took upon him the crown or even governed alone, they, who bore the blame of Clarence's death, would suffer death or at least be ejected from their high estate.

According to common report, the chamberlain Hastings reported all these deliberations by letter and messengers to the Duke of Gloucester, because he had a friendship of long standing with the Duke, and was hostile to the entire kin of the queen.... Besides, it was reported that he had advised the duke to hasten to the capital with a strong force, and avenge the insult done him by his enemies. He might easily obtain his revenge if, before reaching the city, he took the young King Edward under his protection and authority... [The Duke of Gloucester] wrote to the council [declaring that he] had been loyal to his brother Edward, at home and abroad, in peace and war, and would be, if only permitted, equally loyal to his brother's issue.... This letter had a great effect on the minds of the people, who, as they had previously favoured the duke in their hearts from a belief in his integrity, now began to support him openly and aloud; so that it was commonly said by all that the duke deserved the government...

[The] Duke of Gloucester allied himself with the Duke of Buckingham, complaining to the latter of the insult done him by the ignoble family of the queen. Buckingham, since he was of the highest nobility, was disposed to sympathise with another noble; more especially because he had his own reasons for detesting the queen's kin; for, when he was younger, he had been forced to marry the queen's sister, whom he scorned to wed on account of her humble origin...

[Edward V] surrendered himself to the care of his uncle, which was inevitable, for although the dukes [of Gloucester and Buckingham] cajoled him by moderation, yet they clearly showed that they were demanding rather than supplicating...

The queen and the marquis [of Dorset]... perceived that men's minds were not only irresolute but altogether hostile to themselves. Some even said openly that it was more just and profitable that the youthful sovereign should be with his paternal uncle than with his maternal uncles. Comprehending this, the queen and marquis withdrew to... Westminster Abbey [with] the Duke of York [and] the queen's already grown-up daughters.

[The Duke of Gloucester] and the young king entered the city [of London], accompanied by no more than five hundred soldiers drawn partly from his own and partly from the Duke of Buckingham's estates.... As these dukes were seeking at every turn to arouse hatred against the queen's kin, and to estrange public opinion from her relatives, they took special pains to do so on the day they entered the city. For ahead of the procession they sent four wagons loaded with weapons bearing the devices of the queen's brothers and sons, beside criers to make generally known... that these arms had been collected by the duke's enemies... so as to attack and slay the Duke of Gloucester ...

2) Crowland Chronicle
(*Crowland*, pp. 153, 155, 157)

The more farsighted members of the Council thought that the uncles and brothers [of Edward V] on the mother's side should be absolutely forbidden to have control of the person of the young man until he came of age... [Lord Hastings] was afraid that if supreme power fell into the hands of the queen's relatives they would then sharply avenge the alleged injuries done to them by that lord. Much ill-will, indeed, had long existed between Lord Hastings and them. However, the benevolent queen, wishing to extinguish every spark of murmuring and unrest, wrote to her son that he should not have more than 2000 men when he came to London. This number was also pleasing to [Hastings], for he was confident enough, so it seemed, that the Dukes of Gloucester and Buckingham, in whom he had the greatest trust, would bring with them no less a number...

[The] Duke of Gloucester wrote the most pleasant letters to console the queen; he promised to come and offer submission, fealty and all that was due from him to his lord and king Edward V.... Accordingly, he came to York with an appropriate company, all dressed in mourning, and held a solemn funeral ceremony for [Edward IV], full of tears. He bound, by oath, all the nobility of those parts in fealty to [Edward V]; he himself swore first of all.

When he reached Northampton, where the Duke of Buckingham joined him, there arrived to pay their respects Anthony Earl Rivers, the king's maternal uncle, Richard Grey, a very honourable knight, uterine brother to the king, and others.... When first they arrived they were greeted with a particularly cheerful and merry face and, sitting at the duke's table for dinner, they passed the whole time in very pleasant conversation. [Next morning, at Stony Stratford, Gloucester and Buckingham] arrested Earl Rivers, his nephew Richard [and] certain others... and ordered them to be taken to the North in captivity. Immediately after... they rushed into the place where the youthful king was staying and... took prisoner some other servants who were attending him [including] Thomas Vaughan, an aged knight, the prince's chamberlain. The Duke of Gloucester... leader of this conspiracy did not put off or refuse to offer to his nephew, the king, any of the reverence required from a subject.... He said that he was only taking precautions to safeguard his own person because he knew for certain that there were men close to the king who had sworn to destroy his honour and his life...

[When] rumour of this reached London, Queen Elizabeth transferred herself with all her children into the sanctuary of Westminster, [while] you might have seen the partisans of one side and of the other, some sincerely, others dissimulating because of the confusing events, taking this side or that: some collected their associates and stood by at Westminster in the name of the queen, others at London under the protection of Lord Hastings.

A few days later the dukes brought the new king to London to be received in regal style... and they compelled all the lords spiritual and temporal, and the mayor and aldermen of the city of London, to take the oath of fealty to the king. Because this promised best for future prosperity, it was performed with pride and joy by all.

3) John Rous
(Hanham, *Richard III and his Early Historians 1483–1535*, p. 118)

To King Edward IV succeeded, but for a lamentably short time, his son King Edward V, who resided at Ludlow at the time of his father's death.... He was brought up virtuously by virtuous men, remarkably gifted, and very well advanced in learning for his years...

Richard Duke of Gloucester, brother of the dead king and by his ordinance protector of England, came upon him with a strong force at Stony Stratford and took the new king his nephew into his governance by right of his protectorship... Anthony Earl Rivers, elder brother of the queen and the new king's uncle,

Richard Grey, brother of the king on his mother's side, and Sir Thomas Vaughan were removed from their office, forthwith arrested, and sent to be imprisoned in the north at Pontefract, and there shortly after they were unjustly put to death. And so the new king was removed from his loyal servants and received with kisses and embraces, like an innocent lamb falling into the hands of wolves.

4) Polydore Vergil
(*Vergil*, pp. 174, 175, 176)

... the Duke of Gloucester had long conference [with Buckingham at Northampton], insomuch that, as is commonly believed, he even then discovered to Henry his intent of usurping the kingdom...

[At Stony Stratford he] overtook the prince and received him into his rule and government; but he apprehended Anthony [Woodville] and Thomas Vaughan, and divers others, whom after he had taken, supposing that they would not assent to his intent and purpose, he sent back to be kept in ward at Pontefract castle.

[When the news] of so outrageous and horrible [a] fact came to London, all men were wondrously amazed, and in great fear, but especially Elizabeth the queen was much dismayed, and determined forthwith to fly; for, suspecting even then that there was no plain dealing, to the intent she might deliver her other children from the present danger, she conveyed herself with them and the marquis into the sanctuary at Westminster. The very same did other noble men who were of her mind.... But the Lord Hastings who bore privy hatred to the marquis and others of the queen's side, who for that cause had exhorted Richard to take upon him the government of the prince, when he saw all in uproar and that matters fell out otherwise than he had expected, repenting therefore that which he had done, called together to St Paul's church such friends as he knew to be right careful for the life, dignity and estate of Prince Edward, and conferred with them what was best to be done.... Wherefore they concluded to tarry while Duke Richard should come and declare what the matter was, why he had cast them who had the prince in government into prison.... Not long after arrived the Duke Richard and Henry with the prince.... Then did Duke Richard assume the government wholly...

5) Sir Thomas More
(*More*, pp. 10, 11, 15, 16, 19, 20, 21)

[On his deathbed Edward IV] called some of them before him that were at variance, and especially the Lord Marquis Dorset, the Queen's son by her first husband, and Richard, the Lord Hastings, a noble man, then lord chamberlain, against whom the Queen specially grudged for the great favour the King bore him and also for that she thought him secretly familiar with the King in wanton company. Her kindred also bore him so...

[The] Duke of Gloucester soon set afire them that were of themselves easy to kindle, and, in particular two, Edward Duke of Buckingham and Richard Lord Hastings the chamberlain, both men of honour and of great power, the one by long succession from his ancestry, the other by his office and the King's favour, these two, not bearing each to other so much love as both bore hatred unto the Queen's party, in this point accorded together with the Duke of Gloucester that they would utterly remove from the King's company all his mother's friends, under the name of their enemies...

[The Dukes of Gloucester and Buckingham] sent away from the King whom it pleased them and set new servants about him, such as liked better them than him. At which dealing he wept and was nothing content, but it mattered not...

In this wise the Duke of Gloucester took upon himself the order and governance of the young King, whom with much honour and humble reverence he conveyed upward towards the city. But anon the tidings of this matter came hastily to the Queen [who], bewailing her child's ruin, her friends' mischance and her own misfortune, [got] herself in all haste possible with her younger son and her daughters... into the sanctuary...

6

RICHARD OF GLOUCESTER
AS PROTECTOR,
MAY/JUNE 1483

Once firmly established as protector and perhaps, as Mancini suggests, already aiming at 'mastering the throne' itself (1), Richard of Gloucester lost no time in beginning to exercise the extensive powers of political patronage now at his disposal. Close associates like John Lord Howard and Francis Viscount Lovell received advancement, as did Henry Percy Earl of Northumberland, and spectacular rewards certainly came the way of Henry Stafford Duke of Buckingham, no doubt both for services already rendered and as a guarantee of the duke's positive backing in the future should the going get rough: as the *Patent Rolls* and *Harleian Manuscript 433* make clear, Buckingham rapidly became virtually a viceroy in Wales (7). Nevertheless, as Rosemary Horrox has emphasised, Richard's prime objective in May 1483 may well have been to secure continuity with his brother's regime. The Edwardian loyalist John Russell Bishop of Lincoln, possible author of the *Crowland Chronicle*, became chancellor, albeit (if we are to believe John Rous) 'much against his will' (3). Most of Edward IV's former householdmen and servants remained in post, probably a pointer to the continuing political influence and steadying hand of William Lord Hastings, and there were very few changes in the personnel of government (either at national or local level). Even so, by early June 1483, moves might have been afoot, probably involving the Woodvilles and perhaps Hastings too, to curb Richard of Gloucester's power and contain his ambitions. Indeed, when the protector wrote to the city of York on 10 June requesting military assistance (and, significantly, elicited a positive response a few days later), he cited a Woodville conspiracy to 'murder and utterly destroy' himself and Buckingham as urgent justification (8).

If fears were already growing about Gloucester's real intentions early in the month, they must certainly have been given a massive boost by the dramatic events at the Tower of London on 13 June 1483, when the protector not only rid himself of Hastings (as the man most likely to resist any moves to displace Edward V) but also removed a pair of staunch ecclesiastical loyalists (Thomas Rotherham Archbishop of York and John Morton Bishop of Ely) as well. Contemporary and early Tudor sources alike clearly regarded the peremptory arrest and execution of Hastings, portrayed almost invariably as an honourable and upright magnate whose only fault was an unbending commitment to Edward V and his brother, as the ruthless and deliberate act of a man now firmly set on regality for himself. Richard of Gloucester's justification for his behaviour—a rapidly disseminated story alleging the complicity of Hastings and his friends in a conspiracy with the Woodvilles to overthrow him—was widely dismissed as malicious propaganda even at the time (1, 2, 4, 5, 6, 9). Even if Hastings was not nearly so guileless as the Crowland continuator, for one, would have us believe, the chronicler's remark that Gloucester and Buckingham 'did thereafter whatever they wanted' seems amply borne out by the events of the next few days (2). Not only was Elizabeth Woodville forcibly persuaded, by a probably very reluctant Cardinal Thomas Bourchier Archbishop of Canterbury, to allow her younger son Richard of York to leave sanctuary (on 16 June) and join his brother in the Tower (1, 2, 4, 5, 6, 9), but moves were soon instigated too to secure the execution of Rivers, Grey and Vaughan at Pontefract (3) and ensure the imminent presence in London—where, it was reported on 21 June, there 'is much trouble and every man doubts the other'—of more and more provincial partisans of the two dukes (9). Now, with Edwardian loyalists in disarray as a result of Hastings' removal and politicians of all shades of opinion no doubt concerned about their own future well-being, the stage was truly set for the process of usurpation proper to begin.

1) Dominic Mancini
(*Mancini*, pp. 83, 85, 89, 91, 93)

Having entered the city [of London], the first thing [the Duke of Gloucester] saw to was to have himself proclaimed, by authority of the council and all the lords, protector or regent of the king and realm. Then he set his thoughts on removing, or at least undermining, everything that might stand in the way of his mastering the throne...

[The Protector] resolved to get into his power the Duke of York [whom he forsaw] would by legal right succeed to the throne if his brother were removed. To carry through his plan he fixed the date of the coronation; and, as the day drew near, he submitted to the council how improper it seemed that the king should be crowned in the absence of his brother.... Wherefore, he said that, since this boy was held by his mother against his will in sanctuary, he should be liberated [for] this boy wanted to be with his brother. Therefore, with the consent of the council, he surrounded the sanctuary with troops. When the queen saw herself besieged and preparation for violence, she surrendered her son, trusting in the word of the Cardinal of Canterbury that the boy should be restored after the coronation.... At about this time Gloucester gave orders that the son of the Duke of Clarence... should, be kept in confinement in the household of his wife.... For he feared that, if the entire progeny of King Edward [IV] became extinct, yet this child... would still embarrass him.

Having got into his power all the blood royal of the land, yet he considered that his prospects were not sufficiently secure, without the removal or imprisonment of those who had been the closest friends of his brother, and were expected to be loyal to his brother's offspring. In this class he thought to include Hastings, the king's chamberlain; Thomas Rotherham, whom shortly before he had relieved of his office; and the Bishop of Ely.... Therefore the protector rushed headlong into crime, for fear that the ability and authority of these men might be detrimental to him; for he had sounded their loyalty through the Duke of Buckingham, and learnt that sometimes they foregathered in each other's houses. One day these three and several others came to the Tower about ten o'clock to salute the protector, as was their custom. When they had been admitted to the innermost quarters, the protector, as prearranged, cried out that an ambush had been prepared for him, and they had come with hidden arms, that they might be first to open the attack. Thereupon the soldiers, who had been stationed there by their lord, rushed in with the Duke of Buckingham, and cut down Hastings on the false pretext of treason; they arrested the others, whose life, it was presumed, was spared out of respect for religion and holy orders. Thus fell Hastings, killed not by those enemies he had always feared, but by a friend whom he had never doubted. But whom will insane lust for power spare, if it dares violate the ties of kin and friendship? After this execution had been done in the citadel, the townsmen, who had heard the uproar but were uncertain of the cause, became panic-stricken, and each one seized his weapons. But, to calm the multitude, the duke instantly sent a herald to proclaim that a plot had been detected in the citadel, and Hastings, the originator of the plot, had paid the penalty.... At first the ignorant crowd believed, although the real truth was on the lips of many, namely that the plot had been feigned by the duke so as to escape the odium of such a crime...

Thus far, though all the evidence looked as if he coveted the crown, yet there remained some hope, because he was not yet claiming the throne, inasmuch as he still professed to do all these things as an avenger of treasons and old wrongs, and because all private deeds and official documents bore the titles and name of King Edward V.

2) Crowland Chronicle
(*Crowland*, pp. 157, 159)

... Richard Duke of Gloucester received the solemn office which had once fallen to Duke Humphrey of Gloucester who, during the minority of King

Henry [VI], was called protector, of the kingdom. He exercised this authority with the consent and goodwill of all the lords, commanding and forbidding in everything like another king, as occasion demanded. The feast of the Nativity of St John the Baptist [24 June] having been appointed as the day when the king's coronation would take place without fail, everyone hoped for and awaited peace and prosperity in the kingdom. However, a great cause of growing anxiety was the detention in prison of the king's relatives and servants and the fact that the protector did not show sufficient consideration for the dignity and peace of mind of the queen.

Lord Hastings, who seemed to serve these dukes in every way and to have deserved favour of them, bursting with joy over this new World, was asserting that nothing had so far been done except to transfer the government of the kingdom from two blood-relatives of the queen to two nobles of the blood royal and that without any killing.... A very few days after these words, however, grief completely took the place of joy. On the previous day, with remarkable shrewdness, the protector had divided the Council so that, in the morning, part met at Westminster, part in the Tower of London where the king was. On 13 June, the sixth day of the week, when he came to the Council in the Tower, on the authority of the protector, Lord Hastings was beheaded... Thomas Archbishop of York and John Bishop of Ely, saved from capital punishment out of respect for their order, were imprisoned in different castles in Wales. In this way, without justice or judgement, the three strongest supporters of the new king were removed and, with all the rest of his faithful men expecting something similar, these two dukes [Gloucester and Buckingham] did thereafter whatever they wanted.

The following Monday they came by boat to Westminster with a great crowd, with swords and clubs, and compelled the lord cardinal of Canterbury to enter the sanctuary, with many others, to call upon the queen, in her kindness, to allow her son Richard Duke of York to leave and come to the Tower for the comfort of the king his brother. She willingly agreed to the proposal and sent out the boy who was taken by the lord cardinal to the king in the Tower of London.

From that day both these dukes showed their intentions not in private but openly.

3) John Rous
(Hanham, *Richard III and his Early Historians 1483–1535*, pp. 119, 120)

[The Protector] removed the Archbishop of York from the office of chancellor, and Master John Russell, Bishop of Lincoln, former keeper of the privy seal, replaced him, though much against his will.... Shortly after

[Rivers, Grey and Vaughan] were cruelly killed at Pontefract, lamented by almost all and innocent of the deed charged against them, and the Earl of Northumberland, their chief judge, proceeded to London.... And so these lords were condemned to death as if they had in fact plotted the death of Richard Duke of Gloucester... and, for a thing they had never contemplated, the innocent humbly and peaceably submitted to a cruel fate from their enemies' butchers.

4) Great Chronicle of London
(*Great Chronicle*, pp. 230-1)

... the protector, being accompanied by the Archbishop of Canterbury, went unto Westminster and there behaved him so gloriously unto the queen with his manifold dissimulated fair promises that neither she nor yet the archbishop had in them any manner of suspicion of guile. But in good and loving manner, trusting fully it should be for the welfare of the child, delivered unto them the Duke of York...

And all this season the Lord Hastings was had in great favour with the protector and received of him many great benefits and gifts, as many other noble men did, and all to bring his evil purpose about. And... upon the 13th day of June he appointed a Council to be held within the Tower, to which were invited the Earl of Derby, the Lord Hastings, with many others, but most of such as he knew would favour his cause. And upon the same day Lord Hastings dined with him and, after dinner, rode behind him or behind the Duke of Buckingham to the Tower, where, when they with the other lords had entered the council chamber and had communed for a while of such matters as he had previously proposed, suddenly one made an outcry at the council chamber door, 'Treason! treason!', and forthwith the usher opened the door and then pressed in such men as were before appointed and straightway laid hands upon the Earl of Derby and the Lord Hastings; and at once, without any process of law or lawful examination, led Lord Hastings out unto the green beside the chapel and there, upon an end of a squared piece of timber, without any long confession or other space of remembrance, struck off his head. And thus was this noble man murdered for his truth and fidelity which he firmly bore unto his master.... And in like manner would the Earl of Derby have been dealt with, as the fame after went, saving [that the protector] feared the Lord Strange, the earl's son, who was then in Lancashire, wherefore he was immediately set at liberty without hurt, except that his face was grazed a little with some weapon when the tyrants first entered the chamber. Then were the Archbishop of York, Doctor Rotherham, and the Bishop of Ely, Doctor Morton, set in surety for a time...

5) Polydore Vergil
(*Vergil*, pp. 178, 179, 181, 182)

And so was the innocent child [Richard Duke of York] pulled out of his mother's arms...

This done, Richard, whose mind partly was inflamed with desire of usurping the kingdom, partly was troubled by guiltiness of intent to commit so heinous wickedness... thought afterwards nothing better than to mollify the multitude with largesse and liberality, than to win the hearts of his adversaries with gifts, rewards and promises, then in the Tower, where himself and his nephews remained, to consult, confer and deliberate anew with the noble men daily in most crafty and subtle manner...

[Perceiving] that William Lord Hastings was most vehement and earnest to have Prince Edward once crowned king, who chiefly amongst all the nobility was, for his bountifulness and liberality, much beloved of the common people, bearing great sway among all sorts of men and persons of best reputation, whether it were that he feared his power or despaired it possible to draw him to his side and opinion, he determined to rid the man out of the way.... Wherefore, burning with rage incredible to bring to effect the thing which in his mind was resolved, he drew a plot for the Lord Hastings...

William Lord Hastings had scarce leisure to make his confession before his head was struck from his shoulders.... As soon as this deed was done they cried 'Treason, treason' throughout the whole Tower [and] throughout the city the citizens... began to cry out likewise... [Then] began every man on his own behalf to fear... and to look for nothing else but cruel slaughter or miserable flight; and all men generally lamented the death of that man, in whom both they and the nobles who favoured King Edward's children had reposed their whole hope and confidence. Now perceived they well that Duke Richard would spare no man so that he might obtain the kingdom, and that he would convert the regal authority into tyranny.

6) Sir Thomas More
(*More*, pp. 42, 44, 46, 47, 48, 49, 52)

When the lord cardinal and... other lords... had received this young Duke [of York], they brought him into the Star Chamber where the protector took him in his arms and kissed him with these words: 'Now welcome, my Lord, even with all my heart'.... Thereupon forthwith they brought him to the king his brother in the bishop's palace at St Paul's, and from thence through the city honourably into the Tower, out of which, after that day, they never came abroad.

When the protector had both the children in his hands, he opened himself more boldly, both to certain other men and also chiefly to the Duke of Buckingham, although I know that many thought that this duke was privy to all the protector's counsel even from the beginning...

[The] protector and the duke, after they had set the Lord Cardinal, the Archbishop of York, [the] Bishop of Ely, the Lord Stanley and the Lord Hastings, then lord chamberlain, with many other noble men, to commune and devise about the coronation in one place, as fast were they in another place contriving the contrary and to make the protector king...

[On] Friday the thirteenth day of June many lords assembled in the Tower... [The] protector came in among them, first about nine of the clock, saluting them courteously.... And soon after one hour, between ten and eleven, he returned into the chamber among them, all changed, with a wonderfully sour angry countenance, knitting the brows, frowning and fretting and gnawing on his lips... [As] in a great anger, he clapped his fist upon the board a great rap. At which token given, one cried 'Treason!' without the chamber. Therewith a door clapped, and in came there rushing men in armour, as many as the chamber might hold. And at once the protector said to the Lord Hastings, 'I arrest thee, traitor'...

So was [Hastings] brought forth unto the green beside the chapel within the Tower, and his head laid down upon a long log of timber and there struck off...

Thus ended this honourable man, a good knight and a gentle, of great authority with his prince.... A loving man and passing well beloved. Very faithful, and trusty enough, trusting too much.

7) Chancery Patent Rolls/Harleian Manuscript 433: rewards to Henry Stafford Duke of Buckingham, May 1483

(*CPR*, 1476–85, pp. 349-50, 356; *Harleian MSS 433*, Vol. 1, pp. 28-9)

a) *16 May 1483*: grant for life to Henry Duke of Buckingham of the offices of chief justice and chamberlain in South and North Wales, constable of the castles of Carmarthen and Cardigan etc. in etc. in Wales, and the governance and supervision of all the king's subjects in South and North Wales and the Marches.

b) *16 May 1483*: grant to Henry Duke of Buckingham of the supervision and power of array of the king's subjects in the counties of Salop, Hereford, Dorset and Wiltshire.

c) *May 1483*: Henry Duke of Buckingham in office as justice and chamberlain in South Wales; constable and captain of the castle of Aberystwyth, and constable of other castles and towns there, and in Salop and Hereford;

steward of royal castles, lordships, manors etc. in South Wales, the Marches, Salop and Hereford; constable, steward and receiver of the castle, manor and town of Monmouth, and other castles etc. in South Wales, North Wales and the Marches, part of the duchy of Lancaster; constable, steward and receiver of Usk, and other castles, lordships etc. in North Wales, South Wales, the Marches, Salop and Hereford, part of the earldom of March; justice and chamberlain of North Wales, constable and captain of the castle and town of Conway, and other castles in North Wales, etc.

8) York Civic Records
(*York Civic Records*, Vol. 1, pp. 73-4)

a) *Richard of Gloucester to the city of York, 10 June 1483*

... as you love the welfare of us, and the welfare and surety of your own self, we heartily pray you to come to us in London in all the diligence you possibly can, with as many as you can make defensibly arrayed, there to aid and assist us against the queen, her bloody adherents and affinity, who have intended and daily do intend, to murder and utterly destroy us and our cousin, the Duke of Buckingham, and the old royal blood of this realm, and as it is now openly known, by their subtle and damnable ways forecast the same, and also the final destruction and disinheritance of you and all other the inheritors and men in honour, as well of the north parts as other countries, that belong to us...

b) *15 June 1483*

... as much as my lord of Gloucester's good grace has written to the city how that the queen and her adherents intend to destroy his good grace and others of the blood royal, it was agreed that Thomas Wrangwysh [and others], with 200 horsemen, defensibly arrayed, shall ride up to London to assist my said lord's good grace, and to be at Pontefract on Wednesday night next coming, there to attend upon my lord of Northumberland, to go to my said lord of Gloucester's good grace.

9) Stonor Letters, Simon Stallworth to Sir William Stonor, 21 June 1483
(*The Stonor Letters and Papers*, ed. C. L. Kingsford, Vol. 2, p. 161)

... with us is much trouble and every man doubts the other. As on Friday last was the lord chamberlain beheaded soon upon noon. On Monday last was at

Westminster great plenty of harnessed men: there was the deliverance of the Duke of York to my lord cardinal, my lord chancellor and many other lords temporal: and with him met my lord of Buckingham in the midst of the hall of Westminster: my lord protector receiving him at the Star Chamber door with many loving words: and so departed with my lord cardinal to the Tower, where he is, blessed be Jesus, merry.... It is thought there shall be 20,000 of my lord protector's and my lord of Buckingham's men in London this week: to what intent I know not but to keep the peace.... The lord Archbishop of York [and] the Bishop of Ely are yet in the Tower.... All the lord chamberlain's men [are] become my lord of Buckingham's men.

7

THE USURPATION OF RICHARD III, JUNE 1483

The precise circumstances surrounding Richard of Gloucester's seizure of the throne remain somewhat mysterious. Even more difficult to sort out are the particular arguments put forward to justify his behaviour and their validity (if any). The confusion of the sources, moreover, probably reflects a certain indecision and uncertainty as to the best procedure on the part of Gloucester and Buckingham themselves. On Sunday 22 June, ironically enough the day on which Edward V's coronation should have taken place, sermons were preached at St Paul's (by Dr Ralph Shaw, in the presence of the two dukes) and elsewhere calling into question Edward IV's right to rule (and his son's after him) on the grounds that he (Edward IV) was a bastard and urging the validity of Richard of Gloucester's claim to the throne as Richard of York's only legitimate and rightful successor (1, 4, 5, 6). These may well have received a notably cool reception (4, 5, 6), as did a flamboyant speech delivered by Buckingham to leading men of London in the Guildhall on 24 June, nicely related by the probably well-informed *Great Chronicle of London* (4). Perhaps it was in this speech that the famous story of Edward IV's pre-contracted marriage to Eleanor Butler, invalidating his later marriage to Elizabeth Woodville and bastardizing his children by her, received its first public hearing. Just such a case for the protector's becoming king may well have been advanced in an elaborate petition emanating from an assembly which should have been a parliament and presented to Richard of Gloucester on 26 June (1, 2, 7): the pre-contract, as well as the invalidity by reason of his father's attainder of any claim by Clarence's son to the succession, certainly formed the mainstay of a later act of parliament (in January 1484) confirming the new king's title (8).

Responding to the petition (the very production of which may well have reflected fears in London of Gloucester's ruthlessness if checked and the anticipated arrival in the capital of formidable forces from the north and elsewhere), the protector formally accepted the Crown and allowed himself to be conducted to Westminster Hall where he regally took possession of the marble chair (2, 4).

Inevitably, there has been considerable historical debate about these proceedings, particularly the vexed question of the alleged pre-contract. The elaborations in early Tudor sources may well be suspect: Sir Thomas More, for instance, is clearly mistaken in recording Elizabeth Lucy (rather than Eleanor Butler) as Edward IV's rightful spouse (6). Only Philippe de Commines firmly identifies Robert Stillington Bishop of Bath and Wells as Gloucester's prime informant on the matter (3), while the two most nearly contemporary narrative sources—Dominic Mancini and the Crowland continuator—raise as many problems as they solve (1, 2). Nevertheless, the balance of likelihood is that the pre-contract story was a fabrication designed to provide a cover of legality for a blatant act of usurpation. Richard III may have been convinced, of course, that he was indeed serving the interests of the nation—but such, through the ages, has all too frequently been the politician's justification for arbitrary action.

Certainly, once established on the throne, Richard III made hasty preparations for the coronation of himself and his wife Anne, preparations clearly involving a prominent role for his provincial (especially northern) supporters: *en route* to London, indeed, northerners (notably Sir Richard Ratcliffe) supervised on the king's behalf the elimination of Rivers, Grey and Vaughan at Pontefract, perhaps, as the Crowland chronicler remarks, 'without any form of trial' (2). Early in July Richard himself visited his newly arrived forces in their camp to the north of the city of London, and they certainly seem to have been powerfully present on the streets of the capital during the magnificent coronation celebrations of 6 July 1483 (1, 2, 5).

1) Dominic Mancini
(*Mancini*, pp. 95, 97, 99, 101)

When Richard felt secure from all those dangers that at first he feared... he often rode through the capital surrounded by a thousand attendants... as yet under the name of protector.... When he exhibited himself through the streets of the city he was scarcely watched by anybody, rather did they curse him with a fate worthy of his crimes, since no one now doubted at what he was aiming.

After that he took a special opportunity of publicly showing his hand; since he so corrupted preachers of the divine word that in their sermons to the people they did not blush to say, in the face of decency and all religion, that the progeny of King Edward should be instantly rooted out, for neither had he been a legitimate king nor could his issue be so. Edward, they said, was conceived in adultery and was in every way unlike the late Duke of York, whose son he was falsely said to be, but Richard Duke of Gloucester, who altogether resembled his father, was to come to the throne as the legitimate successor.

In the meantime the duke summoned to London all the peers of the realm.... Each came with the retinue that his title and station demanded: but the duke advised them to retain a few attendants... and send back the others to their homes. As a pretext for this he alleged the fear of the London citizens lest so great a concourse of men in a wealthy city might turn to plundering.... They obeyed his instructions and, when the duke saw that all was ready, as though he knew nothing of the affair, he secretly despatched the Duke of Buckingham to the lords to submit to their decision the disposal of the throne. He argued that it would be unjust to crown this boy, who was illegitimate because his father King Edward [IV], on marrying Elizabeth, was legally contracted to another wife to whom ... Warwick had joined him. Indeed, on Edward's authority, [Warwick] had espoused the other lady by proxy... on the continent. Besides, Elizabeth herself had been married to another and had been ravished rather than espoused by Edward, with the result that their entire offspring was unworthy of the kingship. As for the son of the Duke of Clarence, he had been rendered ineligible for the crown by the felony of his father.... The only survivor of the royal stock was Richard Duke of Gloucester, who was legally entitled to the crown, and could bear its responsibilities thanks to his proficiency. His previous career and blameless morals would be a sure guarantee of his good government. Although he would refuse such a burden, he might yet change his mind if he were asked by the peers. On hearing this the lords consulted their own safety, warned by the example of Hastings, and perceiving the alliance of the two dukes, whose power, supported by a multitude of troops, would be difficult and hazardous to resist. [Seeing] themselves surrounded and in the hands of the dukes [they] determined to declare Richard their king...

On the following day all the lords gathered at the house of Richard's mother.... There the whole business was transacted [and] the oaths of allegiance given.... On the two following days the people of London and the higher clergy did likewise.... This being accomplished, a date was fixed for the coronation...

[As] the day appointed for the coronation approached, Richard summoned troops to the number of six thousand into the city from his own estates and those of the Duke of Buckingham. He was afraid lest any uproar should be fomented against him at his coronation.... He himself went out to meet the soldiers before they entered the city; and, when they were drawn up in a circle in a very great field, he passed with bared head around their ranks and thanked them; then, accompanied by the troops, he returned to the city.... The troops being stationed at suitable points, the day arrived preceding the coronation... [The] king on that day left the Tower of London.... Passing through the midst of the city attended by the entire nobility and a display of royal honours, with bared head he greeted all onlookers [and] received their acclamations.... On the following day the Cardinal of Canterbury, albeit unwillingly, anointed and crowned him king of England.

2) Crowland Chronicle
(*Crowland*, pp. 159, 161)

Armed men in frightening and unheard-of numbers were summoned from the North, Wales and other districts within their command and power, and on the 26th day [of] June, Richard, the protector, claimed for himself the government of the kingdom with the name and title of king; and, on the same day, in the great hall of Westminster, he thrust himself into the marble chair. The pretext for this intrusion and taking possession in this way was as follows. It was put forward, by means of a supplication contained in a certain parchment roll, that King Edward's sons were bastards, on the grounds that he had been precontracted to a certain Lady Eleanor Butler before he married Queen Elizabeth and, further, that the blood of his other brother, George Duke of Clarence, had been attainted, so that, at the time, no certain and uncorrupt blood of the lineage of Richard Duke of York could be found except in the person of Richard Duke of Gloucester. At the end of this roll, on behalf of the lords and commonalty of the kingdom, he was entreated to assume his lawful rights. It was put about at the time that this roll originated in the North, whence so many people came to London, although there was no one who did not know the identity of the author, who was in London at the time, of such sedition and infamy.

[A] multitude of such people were moving from the North towards the South under their chief leader and organiser, Sir Richard Ratcliffe, and when they had reached the town of Pontefract, on the orders of this Richard Ratcliffe, Anthony Earl Rivers, Richard Grey [and] Thomas Vaughan were beheaded without any form of trial and in the sight of these same people. This was the second shedding of innocent blood during these sudden changes.

After these events the cardinal Thomas Archbishop of Canterbury, was summoned and, on 6 July following, Richard of Gloucester was anointed and crowned [at] Westminster [Abbey].

3) Philippe de Commines
(*Commines*, pp. 353-4)

... the Bishop of Bath, who had previously been King Edward's chancellor before being dismissed and imprisoned ... revealed to the Duke of Gloucester that King Edward, being very enamoured of a certain English lady, promised to marry her, provided that he could sleep with her first, and she consented. The bishop said that he had married them when only he and they were present.... Later King Edward fell in love again and married the daughter of an English knight, Lord Rivers. She was a widow with two sons... [The bishop] told the Duke of Gloucester all about this affair and helped him a great deal in the execution of his evil plan. The duke had his two nephews murdered and made himself king...

4) Great Chronicle of London
(*Great Chronicle*, pp. 231, 232, 233)

... a crew of men was arrayed in the North and [the protector] commanded them to speed towards London. After this the prince and the Duke of York were held more straitly and then was privy talking in London that the lord protector should be king.

    ... upon the Sunday next following the day of execution of the Lord Hastings, at St Paul's cross, being present the lord protector and the Duke of Buckingham, with a huge audience of [lords] spiritual and temporal, [it] was declared by Doctor Ralph Shaw... that the children of King Edward were not rightful inheritors of the crown, and that King Edward was not the legitimate son of the Duke of York as the lord protector was. By this declaration and many other allegations and opprobrious reports he then alleged that the lord protector was most worthy to be king and no other. This sermon so discontented the greater part of that audience that... after this day [Shaw] was little reputed or regarded...

    Then upon the Tuesday next ensuing ... the Duke of Buckingham came unto the Guildhall, where in readiness for his coming the mayor with his brethren and a fair multitude of citizens were assembled in their liveries. To this assembly the duke then made an oration, rehearsing the great excellency of the lord protector and the manifold virtues which God had endowed him with, and the rightful title which he had to the crown. It lasted a good half hour, and was so well and eloquently uttered and with so angelic a countenance, and every pause and time was so well ordered, that such as heard him marvelled and said that never before that day had they heard any man, learned or unlearned, make such [an] oration as that was. When he had finished and well exhorted the assembly to admit the lord protector for their liege lord and king, and they, to satisfy his mind, more for fear than for love, had cried in small number 'Yea! Yea!', he departed.

    Whereupon the Thursday next ensuing ... the lord protector took possession at Westminster in the Great Hall... seated in the king's chair... Then was hasty provision made for his coronation, so that upon the 6th day of July he and Queen Anne his wife were at one mass solemnly crowned...

5) Polydore Vergil
(*Vergil*, pp. 183, 184, 185, 186, 187)

... being blind with covetousness of reigning, whom no foul fact could now hold back, after he had resolved not to spare the blood of his own house, [Richard] had secret conference with one Ralph Shaw, a divine of great reputation, [to] whom he uttered that his father's inheritance ought to descend to him...

[Richard] came in royal manner, with a great guard of armed men, to the church of St Paul, and there was attentively present at the sermon, in whose hearing Ralph Shaw... began to instruct the people, by many reasons, how the late King Edward was not begotten by Richard Duke of York but by some other [whereas] no one could doubt but Richard... was the duke's true son who by right ought to inherit the realm.... When the people heard these words, they were wondrous vehemently troubled in mind therewith... [Also] there is a common report that King Edward's children were, in that sermon, called bastards, and not King Edward, which is void of all truth; for Cecily, King Edward's mother, being falsely accused of adultery, complained afterwards in sundry places to right many noble men, whereof some yet live, of that great injury which her son Richard had done her...

Now by these means it was thought that Duke Richard had attained the sovereignty, and the same was everywhere so reported, though more for awe than goodwill...

The Duke of Buckingham delivered, in long process [in the Guildhall], Duke Richard's mind, and, on his behalf, declared [the duke's demand of] the kingdom from which he had been defrauded by his brother Edward...

[Richard] commanded forthwith five thousand soldiers which were levied in Yorkshire—for to them he most trusted—to be sent to him under the conduct of Richard Ratcliffe...

And so, having assembled together a company of the nobility, he was created king at Westminster.

6) Sir Thomas More
(*More*, pp. 66, 68)

... it was by the protector and his council concluded that Doctor Shaw should, in a sermon at St Paul's cross, signify to the people that neither King Edward himself nor the Duke of Clarence were lawfully begotten, nor were [they] the very children of the Duke of York, but [were] begotten unlawfully by other persons by the adultery of the duchess their mother. And that also Dame Elizabeth Lucy was verily the wife of King Edward, and so the prince and all his children bastards that were begotten upon the queen...

While these words were being spoken the protector, accompanied by the Duke of Buckingham, went through the people [and then] stood to hearken to the sermon. But the people were so far from crying 'King Richard!' that they stood as if they had been turned into stones, for wonder of this shameful sermon. After which, once ended, the preacher got him home and never after dared look out for shame, but kept him out of sight like an owl...

7) Harleian Manuscript 433
(*Harleian MS 433*, Vol. 3, p. 29)

... now every good true Englishman is bound... to make his oath... and owe his service and fidelity to him that good law, reason and the concordant assent of the lords and commons of the realm have ordained to reign over the people, which is our sovereign lord King Richard III [whose] sure and true title is evidently shown and declared in a bill of petition which the lords spiritual and temporal and the commons of this land solemnly presented to the king's highness at London the 26th day of June. Whereupon the king's highness, notably assisted by well near all the lords spiritual and temporal of this realm, went the same day to his palace of Westminster, and... within the great hall there took possession and declared his mind that the same day he would begin to reign over his people, and from thence rode solemnly to the cathedral church of London and was received there with procession, with great congratulation and acclamation of all the people in every place... that the king was in that day.

8) Rolls of Parliament: Act settling the crown on Richard III and his descendants, 1484
(*Rotuli Parliamentorum*, Vol. VI, pp. 240-2)

... we consider that [in] the reign of King Edward IV, late deceased, after the ungracious pretended marriage... made between King Edward and Elizabeth, sometime wife to Sir John Grey, late naming herself Queen of England, the order of all politic rule was perverted... [Also] we consider that [this] pretended marriage [was] made of great presumption, without the knowledge or assent of the lords of this land ... [The] pretended marriage was made privately and

1. Edward IV, early sixteenth century portrait . (Reproduced by permission of the Society of Antiquaries of London)

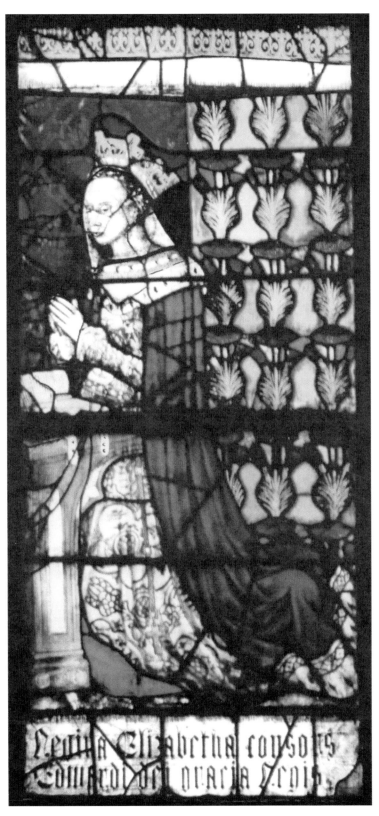

2. Elizabeth Woodville from stained glass in Canterbury Cathedral. (Geoffrey Wheeler)

3. Richard III, portrait painted soon after 1516. (Reproduced by permission of the Society of Antiquaries of London)

4. Fotheringhay Castle. (Julian Rowe)

5. Middleham Castle. (Geoffrey Wheeler)

6. Tomb of the Duke and Duchess of York erected by Elizabeth I in Fotheringhay Church. (Geoffrey Wheeler)

7. Richard Neville, Earl of Warwick, as a weeper on the tomb of his father in law Richard Beauchamp, Earl of Warwick. (Geoffrey Wheeler)

8. The battle of Barnet, redrawn from the Ghent Manuscript. (Geoffrey Wheeler)

9. The battle of Tewkesbury, redrawn from the Ghent manuscript. (Geoffrey Wheeler)

10. Garter stall plate of the Duke of Clarence. (Geoffrey Wheeler)

11. Garter stall plate of Lord Hastings, (Geoffrey Wheeler)

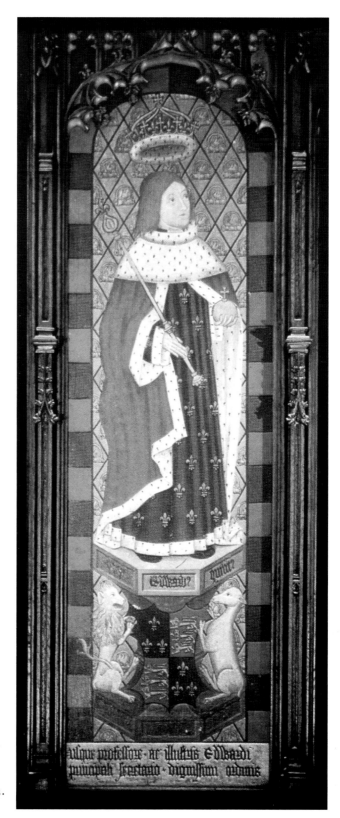

12. Edward V, from the painting on the Chantry screen of Bishop Oliver King, St George's Chapel, Windsor, c.1503. (Geoffrey Wheeler)

OFFER OF
THE KINGSHIP
TO RICHARD
DVKE of GLOWCESTER
AT BAYNARD'S CASTLE
IVNE 26th
1483

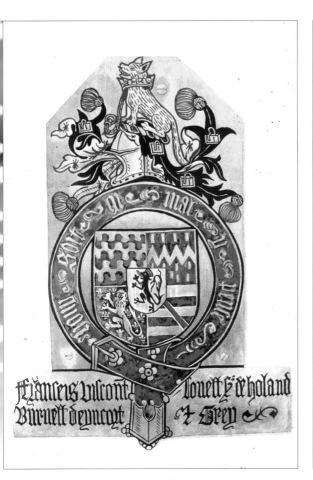

Above left: **14.** Garter stall plate of Viscount Lovell. (Geoffrey Wheeler)

Above right: **15.** Brass of William Catesby, redrawn from a rubbing. (Geoffrey Wheeler)

Opposite: **13.** The Duke of Gloucester accepting the crown in Baynard's Castle, June 1483, from the painting in the Royal Exchange, London. (Geoffrey Wheeler)

16. Richard III, his wife Anne Neville and their son Edward, redrawn from the Rous Roll. (Geoffrey Wheeler)

17. Crowland Abbey. (Geoffrey Wheeler)

18. Pulpit of Fotheringhay Church with the royal arms of Edward IV and the heraldic badges of the Duke of Gloucester (a boar) and the Duke of Clarence (a black bull). (Geoffrey Wheeler)

19. Henry VII, portrait of about 1501. (Reproduced by permission of the Society of Antiquaries of London)

Right: 20. Mediaeval halberd. (Geoffrey Wheeler)

Below: 21. Bones of Richard III. (Reproduced by permission of the University of Leicester)

22. Reconstructed face of Richard III. (Reproduced by permission of the Richard III Society)

secretly, without the issuing of banns, in a private chamber, a profane place...
[At] the time of contract of the same pretended marriage, and before and long
time after, King Edward was and stood married and troth-pledged to one
Dame Eleanor Butler, daughter of the old Earl of Shrewsbury, with whom
King Edward had made a precontract of marriage, a long time before he made
the pretended marriage... [It] appears and follows evidently that King Edward
[and] Elizabeth lived together sinfully and damnably in adultery [and] that all
the issue and children of King Edward are bastards unable to inherit or claim
anything by inheritance...

Moreover... George Duke of Clarence, brother to King Edward, [was]
convicted and attainted of high treason, by reason whereof all [his] issue...
was and is disabled and debarred of all right and claim... they might have...
to the crown and royal dignity of this realm...

Beyond this, we consider that you are the undoubted son and heir of Richard
late Duke of York, truly inheritor to the crown and dignity royal...

8

RICHARD III'S EARLY MONTHS AS KING, JUNE–OCTOBER 1483

Richard III's seizure of the throne in late June 1483 did not arouse much enthusiasm in London nor, seemingly, in southern England generally: yet, if he were to prosper, he clearly needed to project himself successfully as king of the whole nation. Hence the magnificence of his coronation on 6 July, where he paid particular attention to regal tradition, processing ceremonially from the Tower to Westminster, creating knights of the bath, and ensuring his anointing, solemn oath and crowning were in accordance with past liturgical practice (1). Even so, his sense of insecurity is perhaps indicated by the wording of the oath of fealty sworn by the nobility (2) and the fact that northerners, present in large numbers at the coronation celebrations, soon began to enjoy the fruits of his patronage (4). So too did close associates and backers such as Henry Stafford Duke of Buckingham, John Howard, newly created Duke of Norfolk, and Francis Viscount Lovell (3, 8). Nevertheless, most Edwardian loyalists, whatever their inner thoughts on Richard III's recent behaviour might have been, continued (for the time being) to serve him both at the centre and in the shires: in fact, government was very much business as usual.

A fortnight after the coronation, the king and his court embarked on a major progress, no doubt designed both to consolidate Richard's support (especially in the north) and widen the appeal of his regime. His early itinerary included Oxford (where he attended scholastic disputations), Woodstock, Gloucester (where he graciously acceded to the city's request for a charter), Worcester, and Warwick where he was joined by the queen and may have met John Rous: moreover Rous, even in his generally critical post–1485 assessment of the king, remarked that when offered money 'by the peoples of London, Gloucester and Worcester, he declined [it] with thanks, affirming that he would rather have their love than their treasure' (3). Thomas Langton Bishop of St David's, who was in Richard's entourage during this tour, was certainly most impressed by the king's behaviour and the promise it held for the future (6). Progressing next to Coventry and Leicester, the king then struck north via Nottingham and Pontefract to the city of York where he was magnificently received on 29 August 1483 (1, 3, 5, 7a, b).

As the Crowland continuator recorded, Richard III was particularly anxious to create a good impression in his crucial northern power base, not only entertaining lavishly in the city of York and investing his son Edward as Prince of Wales in the minster there, but also granting the city a relief of almost half the taxes it normally paid to the crown (1, 7c). Polydore Vergil, however, believed that his motives were suspect to say the least (5) and, even if Richard's intentions were as honourable and generous as he proclaimed, he may well have been unwise to spend so long away from southern England and the home counties during these critical early weeks of the reign: certainly, moves against him were soon being mooted in the south and west and, as he at last made his way southwards again, he heard (at Lincoln on 11 October) that rebellion had broken out.

1) Crowland Chronicle
(*Crowland*, p. 161)

[The] cardinal, Thomas Archbishop of Canterbury, was summoned and, on 6 July following, Richard of Gloucester received the gift of the royal unction and the crowning in the conventional church of St Peter at Westminster [Westminster Abbey] and at the same time his wife, Queen Anne, received her crown. From that day, while he lived, this man was called King Richard, the third after the Conquest.

Wishing to display [his] superior royal rank as diligently as possible in the North, where he had spent most of his time previously, he left the royal city of London and, passing through Windsor, Oxford and Coventry, came at length to York. There, on a day appointed for the repetition of his crowning in the metropolitan church, he presented his only son, Edward, whom, that same day, he had created Prince of Wales [and] arranged splendid and highly expensive feasts and entertainments to attract to himself the affection of many people. There was no shortage of treasure then to implement the aims of his so elevated mind since, as soon as he first thought about his intrusion into the kingship, he seized everything that his deceased brother, the most glorious King Edward, had collected with the utmost ingenuity and the utmost industry...

2) Oath of Fealty sworn by the peerage at Richard III's Coronation
(Hicks, *Richard III The Man Behind the Myth*, p. 118)

I become true and faithful liegeman unto my sovereign lord King Richard III by the grace of God King of England [and] to his heirs Kings of England and to him and them my faith and truth shall bear during my natural life, and with him and in his cause and quarrel at all times shall take his part and be ready to live and die against all earthly creatures and utterly endeavour me to the resistance and suppression of his enemies, rebels and traitors if I shall know any to the uttermost of my power, and no thing court that in any way may be hurting to his noble and royal person.

3) John Rous
(Hanham, *Richard III and his Early Historians 1483–1535*, p. 122)

... when he was crowned with his queen [Richard] made new lords: Henry Duke of Buckingham was made great chamberlain and steward of England; John Howard, Duke of Norfolk; his son and heir, Earl of Surrey; William Lord Berkeley, Earl of Nottingham and marshal of England; and Lord Lovell, the king's chamberlain.

When King Edward V had been imprisoned, King Richard III gave all his treasure to Henry Duke of Buckingham, who then distributed his livery of Stafford knots and boasted that he had as many of them as Richard Neville Earl of Warwick had formerly had of ... 'ragged staves'. But they were greatly inferior in numbers, and it was not long before the underlying hatred between the king and the duke began to grow.

The king removed to Oxford, and to Woodstock, where by popular request he disafforested a great area of the country.... From there he went to Gloucester, and, for the ancient title of his dukedom, instituted a mayor and aldermen there. And then he went to Worcester, and finally Warwick, where the queen joined him from Windsor.... There were then with the king at Warwick the Bishops of Worcester, Coventry, Lichfield, Durham and St Asaph's; the Duke of Albany, brother of the King of Scotland; Edward Earl of Warwick; Thomas Earl of Surrey, steward of the king's household; the Earl of Huntingdon; John Earl of Lincoln; and the Lords Stanley, Dudley, Morley and Scrope; Francis Lord Lovell, the king's chamberlain, and William Hussy, chief justice of England, and many other lords. And ladies of similar rank with the queen. From here, after a stay of a week, the king moved to Coventry, Leicester, Nottingham and Pontefract, where he instituted a mayor. Then he came to York where [his] little son and heir... was knighted and made Prince of Wales...

4) Great Chronicle of London
(*Great Chronicle*, pp. 233-4)

[After the coronation] the king sent home the lords into their countries, holding with him still the Earl of Derby for a season. And also unto such as went home he gave strait commandments that they should see the countries where they dwelt well guided and that no extortions were done to his subjects. And thus he taught others to exercise justice and goodness which he would not do himself...

The king, with large rewards given to the northern men whom he had sent for [at the time of] his coronation, numbered at 4 or 5 thousand men, he sent them home again; of whom some, bearing them bold of the king's favour, after they had rested them there awhile, began to make such masteries that the king was fain to ride thither himself, where at his coming he put some in execution and so pacified that country and returned again to London.

And shortly after he created his legitimate son Prince of Wales, and his bastard son he made captain of Calais.

Then King Richard, that during this time had spent and largely given away the treasure and goods of King Edward to purchase him friends, was then constrained to seek his friends and to attempt them in borrowing great sums of money...

5) Polydore Vergil
(*Vergil*, pp. 188, 190, 192)

[At York Richard III] was joyfully received of the citizens, who for his coming made certain days public and open triumph... [When] the day of general procession was at hand, [there] was great confluence of people, for desire of beholding the new king. In which procession very solemnly set forth and celebrated by the clergy, the king was present in person, adorned with a notably rich diadem, and accompanied with a great number of noble men; the queen followed also with a crown upon her head, who led by the hand her son Edward, crowned also with so great honour, joy and congratulation of the inhabitants, as in show of rejoicing they extolled King Richard above the skies...

[The king] began afterwards to take on hand a certain new form of life, and to give the show and countenance of a good man, whereby he might be accounted more righteous, more mild, better affected to the commonalty, and more liberal, especially towards the poor. [And so that he] first might merit pardon for his offences at God's hand, then after appease partly the envy of man and procure himself goodwill, he began many works as well public as private.... He founded a college at York of a hundred priests. Also he began now to give ear to the good admonition of his friends. But anon after it appeared evident that fear, which seldom causes continuance of dutiful dealing, made King Richard so suddenly good, forasmuch as the bountifulness of the man, being but counterfeit, waxed cold again quickly...

6) Christ Church Letters, Thomas Langton Bishop of St David's to the Prior of Christ Church, September 1483
(Hanham, *Richard III and his Early Historians 1483–1535*, p. 50)

... I trust to God soon, by Michaelmas, the king shall be at London. He contents the people wherever he goes better than ever did any prince; for many a poor man that has suffered wrong many days has been relieved and helped by him and his commands in his progress. And in many great cities and towns were great sums of money given to him which he has refused. On my faith I never liked the qualities of any prince as well as his; God has sent him to us for the welfare of us all.

7) York Civic Records
(*York Civic Records*, Vol. 1, pp. 78, 79, 82)

a) *John Kendall, King's Secretary, in Nottingham, to the city of York, 23 August 1483*... the king's grace is in good health, and in likewise the queen's grace, and in all their progress have been worshipfully received with pageants; and his lords and judges sitting in every place, determining the complaints of poor folk with due punishment of offenders against his laws... I truly know the king's mind and entire affection that his grace bears towards you and your worshipful city, for your many kind and loving deservings shown to his grace heretofore, which his grace will never forget, and intends therefore so to do unto you that all the kings that ever reigned over you did never so much, doubt not hereof... I advise you to receive him and the queen as honourably as your wisdoms can imagine... as well with pageants [and] such good speeches as can well be devised ... for there come many southern lords and men of worship with them which will mark greatly your receiving [of] their graces...

b) *29 August 1483*

... it was agreed that [the] king shall be presented at his coming with 100 marks in a pair of basins of silver gilt or in a cup of gold... and that [the] queen shall be presented with 100 of gold in a piece...

c) *17 September 1483*

[The king] openly rehearsed the service done [by the city] to his good grace, and also the decay and great poverty of the city, [and] of his most special good grace, without any petition or asking of anything, [he] most graciously and abundantly granted and gave in relief of the city... yearly for ever £58/11/2d...

and over that most graciously granted to the mayor and commonalty of the city yearly £40 for ever...

8) Chancery Patent Rolls: some significant early appointments of Richard III
(*CPR, 1476–85*, pp. 358, 360, 361, 362, 363, 364, 365, 360)

a) *Henry Stafford Duke of Buckingham*

15 July 1483: constable of England; chief justice and chamberlain in South and North Wales etc.; constable and steward of all the king's castles, lordships etc. in Salop and Hereford, with supervision and power of array of all the king's subjects in those counties.

b) *John Howard Duke of Norfolk*

28 June 1483: marshal of England
30 June 1483: steward of England at the king's coronation
16 July 1483: supervision and array of the king's subjects in the counties of Norfolk, Suffolk, Essex, Hertford, Middlesex, Kent, Sussex, Surrey, Berks, Buckingham, Bedford, Cambridge and Huntingdon
25 July 1483: admiral of England, Ireland and Aquitaine

c) *Francis Viscount Lovell*

14 August 1483: king's chamberlain and chief butler of England

d) *Robert Brackenbury Esquire*
17 July 1483: constable of the Tower of London

e) *William Catesby Esquire*
30 June 1483: chancellor of the Exchequer; chancellor of the earldom of March

9

THE FATE OF THE PRINCES
IN THE TOWER

No one will ever know for certain when, or even whether, Richard III had his nephews, the deposed Edward V and his brother Richard of York, murdered in the Tower of London. Sir Thomas More, certainly, presents an elaborate and dramatic account, powerfully loaded against Richard: yet, while claiming at one point that it was 'very truth' and 'well known' that Sir James Tyrell (facing death for treason against Henry VII in 1502) confessed to the murder of the princes, even More admits to drawing on rumours circulating in the early sixteenth century (18). Polydore Vergil provides a similar story, more concisely and with less circumstantial detail, but, while mentioning that Tyrell might have been the princes' murderer, makes no reference to any confession (17). Moreover, even if Tyrell did confess, no such confession has ever been found. London chroniclers writing in early Tudor times, like Vergil and More, were inclined to take on board strong rumours of Richard's responsibility for his nephews' deaths (13, 14, 15); John Rous was firmly convinced of his guilt (11); and an entry in the Anlaby cartulary, probably written shortly after Henry VII's death in April 1509, even suggests (albeit, without supplying the murderer's name) that Edward V was killed *before* Richard III seized the throne (16). Ricardians are inclined to dismiss all such post-1485 writers as mere retailers of Tudor propaganda and unsubstantiated rumour. Yet this will not do: Rous was writing very soon after Richard's death, the London chroniclers did draw on earlier material, and even Vergil and More must have built on a firm basis of existing popular belief about the last Plantagenet king and the fate of his nephews.

Perhaps not surprisingly, more nearly contemporary sources provide relatively little evidence on the matter. George Cely, an English merchant, heard rumours in June 1483 (prior to Gloucester's becoming king) that Edward V might be facing death if not already dead (1), but a reference to 'Edward Bastard' in *Harleian Manuscript 433* suggests he was still alive in mid-July (2a). Another entry in the same source to the 'lord Bastard', dated early March 1485, *might* refer to the younger of the two boys but probably refers to Richard's bastard son John (2b). What is clear is that the princes had disappeared from view by early July 1483, as Dominic Mancini reports: indeed, Mancini heard rumours of Edward V's death before he left London, rumours he felt unable either to confirm or deny (6), and rumours presumably not so widely believed as to prevent a still-born plot to liberate the youngsters from captivity before the month was out (3). Robert Ricart, recorder of Bristol, entered news of their deaths, however, in his *Kalendar* under the mayoral year 1482/3 (4), while Continental commentators soon latched on to stories of their murder: Caspar Weinrich, a citizen of Danzig, reported Richard III's responsibility for their demise in his contemporary annals (5); Guillaume de Rochefort, chancellor of France, took a similar line when addressing the Estates-General at Tours in January 1484 (7); and Diego de Valera had no doubts either in March 1486 (8). Philippe de Commines, by contrast, hedged his bets, apportioning blame to Henry Stafford Duke of Buckingham as well as the king (12); recently discovered, and perhaps contemporary, London jottings similarly point an accusing finger at Buckingham (10); and at least another couple of surviving fragments put him in the frame as well. The Crowland continuator, as so often, is enigmatic (and much depends on how one particular word in the Latin text is translated), but he probably is hinting at Richard III's guilt and may, indeed, have known more than he chose to reveal (9). Bones discovered in a box buried beneath a staircase in the White Tower in 1674 may or may not be those of the princes (19): even if they are, as seems possible (but, as yet, unproven), and even if they can be shown to have encountered violent treatment (more difficult), the identity of their killer (if they were killed!) cannot conclusively be established from them.

Clearly, then, the available evidence, of whatever character, is inconclusive. A case of sorts can be constructed against Buckingham, even if not (despite the efforts of Sir Clements R. Markham and others) against Henry VII. Yet it is surely significant that, even during Buckingham's rebellion (when producing them could have scotched widespread reports in southern England that they were dead), the princes remained firmly hidden from view; and even more significant, perhaps, that their mother Elizabeth Woodville ended up supporting a movement designed to put Henry Tudor Earl of Richmond on the throne (suggesting that, by October 1483, she had given up all hope that her sons were still alive). Of course, they might simply have died of natural causes (not very convincing) or even have been freed (by Henry VII if not Richard III) on condition they lived thereafter in obscurity (not convincing at all). The best presumption, however, must surely be that the Princes in the Tower had met a violent end by early October 1483—an end sanctioned by their uncle as the culminating act of several months spent in a ruthless pursuit of personal security and political power.

1) Cely Memorandum, June 1483
(Hicks, *Richard III: The Man Behind the Myth*, p. 93)

If the King, God save his life, were to die; the Duke of Gloucester were in any peril. If my Lord Prince, whom God protect, were troubled.

2) Harleian Manuscript 433
(*Harleian MS 433*, Vol. 2, pp. 2, 211)

a) *18 July 1483*: warrant authorising payment of wages to fourteen named men for their services to Edward IV and to 'Edward Bastard late called King Edward the Vth'.

b) *9 March 1485*: warrant to Henry Davy 'to deliver to John Goddeslande, footman unto the lord Bastard, two doublets of silk, one jacket of silk, one gown of cloth and two bonnets'.

3) *Richard III to the chancellor, Bishop Russell of Lincoln, 29 July 1483*
(Tudor-Craig, *Richard III*, p. 98)

... whereas we understand that certain persons of such as of late had taken upon them the fact of an enterprise, as we doubt not you have heard, be attached and in ward, we desire and will you that you do make our letters of commission to such persons as by you and our council shall be advised for to sit upon them and to proceed to the due execution of our laws in that behalf...

4) Robert Ricart's Kalendar
(Pollard, *Richard III and the Princes in the Tower*, p. 122)

... in this year [the year ending 15 September 1483] the two sons of King Edward were put to silence in the Tower of London.

5) Caspar Weinrich of Danzig
(*Richard III. A Medieval Kingship*, ed. J. Gillingham, p. 17)

After Easter [1483] King Edward died in England. Later this summer Richard the king's brother seized power and had his brother's children killed and the queen secretly put away...

In the year [1485] in the summer King Richard of England, who had had his brother's children killed, was himself killed...

6) Dominic Mancini
(*Mancini*, p. 93)

... after Hastings was removed, all the attendants who had waited upon the king were debarred access to him. He and his brother were withdrawn into the inner apartments of the Tower proper, and day by day began to be seen more rarely behind the bars and windows, till at length they ceased to appear altogether. The physician Argentine, the last of his attendants whose services the king enjoyed, reported that the young king, like a victim prepared for sacrifice, sought remission of his sins by daily confession and penance, because he believed that death was facing him... I have seen many men burst into tears and lamentations when mention was made of him after his removal from men's sight; and already there was a suspicion that he had been done away with. Whether, however, he has been done away with, and by what manner of death, so far I have not at all discovered.

7) Guillaume de Rochefort, chancellor of France, to the Estates-General at Tours, 15 January 1484
(*England under the Yorkists*, ed. I. D. Thornley, pp. 123-4)

Look [at] what has happened in [England] since the death of King Edward [IV]: how his children, already big and courageous, have been put to death with impunity, and the royal crown transferred to their murderer by the favour of the people.

8) Diego de Valera to the Catholic Monarchs of Castile and Aragon, 1 March 1486
(Tudor-Craig, *Richard III*, p. 68)

... it is sufficiently well known to your royal majesty that this Richard killed two innocent nephews of his to whom the realm belonged after his brother's life; but, for all that King Edward their father was waging war in Scotland, while Richard stayed in England, it is alleged that there he had them murdered with poison.

9) Crowland Chronicle
(*Crowland*, pp. 163, 185)

[During Richard III's post-coronation progress] the two sons of King Edward remained in the Tower of London with a specially appointed guard. In order to release them from such captivity the people of the South and West of the kingdom began to murmur greatly, to form assemblies and to organise associations.... There was also a rumour that those men who had fled to sanctuaries had advised that some of the king's daughters should leave Westminster in disguise and go overseas so that if any human fate, inside the Tower, were to befall the male children, nevertheless through the saving of the daughters the kingdom might some day return to the rightful heirs...

When at last the people [in the south and west] began considering vengeance, public proclamation having been made that Henry Duke of Buckingham... being repentant of what had been done would be captain-in-chief in this affair, a rumour arose that King Edward's sons, by some unknown manner of violent destruction, had met their fate...

[Considering] what befell all three kings who after the Conquest of England were called Richard, a certain poet left these lines in his works:

> There were three Richards.... The third, after exhausting
> the quite ample store of Edward's wealth, was not
> content until he suppressed his brother's progeny and proscribed their
> supporters...

10) Historical Notes of a London Citizen
(*English Historical Review*, Vol. 96, 1981, p. 588)

... this year [1483] King Edward V, late called Prince of Wales, and Richard Duke of York his brother, King Edward IV's sons, were put to death in the Tower 'be the vise' [i.e. by the advice/design] of the Duke of Buckingham.

11) John Rous
(Hanham, *Richard III and his Early Historians 1483–1535*, pp. 120-1)

[Richard] imprisoned his lord King Edward V... together with his brother Richard... [It] was afterwards known to very few by what manner of death they had suffered. The usurper King Richard III then ascended the throne of the slaughtered children.... He received his lord King Edward V blandly, with

embraces and kisses, and within about three months or a little more he killed
him together with his brother...

12) Philippe de Commines
(*Commines*, pp. 89, 354, 397)

On the death of Edward [IV], his second brother the Duke of Gloucester killed
Edward's two sons, declared his daughters bastards and had himself crowned
king...

   [The Earl of Richmond] defeated and killed in battle the cruel King Richard
who shortly before had had his nephews murdered...

   The Duke [of Gloucester] had his two nephews murdered and made himself
king...

   King Richard did not last long; nor did the Duke of Buckingham, who
had put the two children to death, for a few days later King Richard had
Buckingham put to death.

13) Vitellius AXVI
(*Vitellius AXVI*, p. 191)

... anon as the said King Richard had put to death the lord chamberlain and
other gentlemen... he also put to death the two children of King Edward, for
which cause he lost the hearts of the people. And thereupon many gentlemen
intended his destruction.

14) Great Chronicle of London
(*Great Chronicle*, pp. 234, 236-7)

And during this mayor's year [i.e. Sir Edmund Shaw, whose mayoralty ended
28 October 1483] the children of King Edward were seen shooting and
playing in the garden of the Tower at sundry times. All the winter season of
this mayor's time [i.e. Robert Billesdon, October 1483 to October 1484] the
land was in good quiet, but after Easter there was much whispering among
the people that the king had put the children of King Edward to death...

   Word sprang quickly of [Henry Tudor who] made speedy provision to come
to England to claim the crown as his right, considering the death of King
Edward's children, of whom as then men feared not only to say that they were
rid out of this world. But of the manner of their deaths were many opinions,
for some said they were murdered between two feather beds, some said they

were drowned in malmsey, and some said they were pierced with a venomous poison. But howsoever they were put to death, certain it was that before that day they were departed from this world, of which cruel deed Sir James Tyrell was reported to be the doer, but others put weight upon an old servant of King Richard's named...

15) Fabian's Chronicle
(*Fabian*, p. 670)

In this year [1483/4] the foresaid grudge increasing, and the more forasmuch as the common fame went that King Richard had within the Tower put unto secret death the two sons of his brother Edward IV, for the which, and other causes had within the breast of the Duke of Buckingham, the said duke, in secret manner, conspired against him...

16) Anlaby Cartulary
(*Richard III: A Medieval Kingship*, ed. J. Gillingham, p. 54)

Edward V died on 22 June; he reigned 2 months and 8 days but was not crowned. He was killed and nobody knows where he is buried.

17) Polydore Vergil
(*Vergil*, pp. 187-90)

[Richard] determined by death to despatch his nephews because so long as they lived he could never be out of hazard; wherefore he sent warrant to Robert Brackenbury, lieutenant of the Tower of London, to procure their death with all diligence by some convenient means... [But] after he had received the king's horrible commission, [he] was astonished with the cruelty of the fact, and fearing lest if he should obey the same [it] might at one time or other turn to his own harm, [and] did therefore defer the doing thereof in the hope that the king would spare his own blood, or their tender age, or alter that heavy determination ... [When] Richard understood the lieutenant to make delay of that which he had commanded, he anon committed the charge of hastening that slaughter unto... James Tyrell who, being forced to do the king's commandment, rode sorrowfully to London, and, to the worst example that has almost ever been heard of, murdered those babes of the royal issue.

This end had Prince Edward and Richard his brother; but with what kind of death these children were executed is not certainly known. But King Richard, delivered by this fact from his care and fear, kept the slaughter not long secret, who, within a few days after, permitted the rumour of their death to go abroad, to the intent, as we may well believe, that after the people understood no male issue of King Edward to be now left alive, they might with better mind and goodwill bear and sustain his government. But when the fame of this notable foul act was dispersed through the realm, so great grief struck generally to the hearts of all men, that the same, subduing all fear, they wept everywhere.... What man is there in this world who, if he has regard to such noble children thus shamefully murdered, will not tremble and quake...

18) Sir Thomas More
(*More*, pp. 83-6)

... I shall rehearse you the dolorous end of those babes, not after every way that I have heard, but after that way that I have so heard by such men and by such means as methinks it were hard but it should be true.

... forasmuch as his mind gave him that, his nephews living, men would not reckon that he could have right to the realm, [Richard] thought therefore without delay to be rid of them, as though the killing of his kinsmen could amend his cause and make him a kindly king.

Whereupon he sent one John Green, whom he specially trusted, unto Sir Robert Brackenbury, constable of the Tower, with a letter and credence also, that the same Sir Robert should... put the two children to death... who plainly answered that he would never put them to death... with which answer John Green, returning, recounted the same to King Richard at Warwick...

[On] the morrow he sent [Sir James Tyrell] to Brackenbury with a letter, by which he was commanded to deliver [to] Sir James all the keys of the Tower for one night, to the end he might there accomplish the king's pleasure.... After which letter delivered and the keys received, Sir James appointed the night next ensuing to destroy them...

[Sir] James Tyrell devised that they should be murdered in their beds. To the execution whereof he appointed Miles Forest, one of the four that kept them, a fellow fleshed in murder beforetime. To him he joined one John Dighton, his own horsekeeper, a big broad square strong knave. Then, all the others being removed from them, this Miles Forest and John Dighton, about midnight, the innocent children lying in their beds, came into the chamber and suddenly lapped them up among the clothes, so bewrapped them and entangled them, keeping down by force the featherbed and pillows hard unto their mouths, that within a while smothered and stifled, their breath failing, they gave up to God their innocent souls into the joys of heaven, leaving to the tormentors their bodies dead in the bed. After the wretches perceived them, first by the struggling with the pains of death, and after long lying still, to be thoroughly dead, they laid their bodies naked out upon the bed and fetched Sir James to see them. Who, upon the sight of them, caused those murderers to bury them at the stair foot, meetly deep in the ground under a great heap of stones.

Then rode Sir James in great haste to King Richard, and showed him all the manner of the murder, who gave him great thanks and, as some say, there made him knight. But he allowed not, as I have heard, the burying in so vile a corner, saying that he would have them buried in a better place because they were a king's sons.... Whereupon they say that a priest of Sir Robert Brackenbury took up the bodies again and secretly interred them in such place as, by the occasion of his death, who alone knew it, could never after come to light. Very truth it is and well known that at such time as Sir James Tyrell was in the Tower, for treason committed against the most famous prince King Henry the Seventh, both Dighton and he were examined, and confessed the murder in manner above-written, but whither the bodies were removed they could nothing tell.

And thus, as I have learned from them that much knew and little cause had to lie, were these two noble princes, these innocent tender children, born of most royal blood, brought up in great wealth, likely long to live to reign and rule in the realm, by traitorous tyranny taken, deprived of their estate, shortly shut up in prison, and privily slain and murdered, their bodies cast God knows where, by the cruel ambition of their unnatural uncle and his pitiless tormentors.

19) Francis Sandford, 1707
(Sandford, *A Genealogical History of the Kings and Queens of England*, pp. 427-429)

Till upon Friday the ... day of July Anno 1674 (taking this relation from a gentleman, an eyewitness, and principally concerned in the whole scrutiny) in order to the rebuilding of the several offices in the Tower, and to clear the White Tower from all contiguous buildings, digging down the stairs which led from the King's lodgings, to the Chapel in the said Tower, about ten feet in the ground were found the bones of two striplings in (as it seemed) a wooden chest, which upon the survey were found proportionable to the ages of those two brothers *viz.* about thirteen and eleven years. The skull of the one being entire, the other broken, as were indeed many of the other bones, as also the chest, by the violence of the labourers, who not being sensible of what they had in hand, cast the rubbish and them away together, wherefore they were caused to sift the rubbish and by that means preserved all the bones.

The circumstances from the story being considered ... this matter was reported to the king. Upon the presumptions that these were the bones of the said Princes his Majesty King Charles II was graciously pleased to command, that the said bones should be put into a marble urn and deposited among the reliques of the royal family in the chapel of King Henry VII in Westminster Abbey.

10

BUCKINGHAM'S REBELLION,
OCTOBER 1483

During the autumn of 1483 Richard III had to cope with a rebellion of major proportions in the southern counties of England, a rebellion involving substantial numbers of gentry (including many of the leaders of county society), and a rebellion clearly showing the extent of resentment and mistrust already engendered by the new king's rule. Most seriously, Buckingham's rebellion (as it is, traditionally and misleadingly, often called) graphically highlighted the failure of Richard's policy of winning over, and continuing in office, most of Edward IV's former householdmen and servants, men who up to now had seemed loyal to him. Part of the explanation, perhaps, lies in already present suspicions among former Edwardian loyalists of members of the king's pre-1483 ducal affinity and backers of his usurpation, especially northerners, who appeared to enjoy terms of particular intimacy with him (although their political and social advancement on a considerable scale, whether in the royal household, central administration or shires beyond their normal spheres of influence, was a result rather than a cause of the October rebellion). Fears regarding the fate of the Princes in the Tower played a significant role as well (not least in explaining Elizabeth Woodville's involvement). And then, of course, there is the puzzling behaviour of Henry Stafford Duke of Buckingham (hitherto Richard's closest and most spectacularly rewarded supporter). Ominously, too, Henry Tudor Earl of Richmond first emerged, at the same time, as a potentially serious rival, especially once his possible marriage to Edward IV's eldest daughter Elizabeth of York was mooted.

Initially, if we are to believe the Crowland chronicler, the rebels' prime objective was to deliver Edward V and his brother from captivity; only when rumours spread of their deaths did men's thoughts turn to the alternative possibility of replacing Richard III by Henry Tudor Earl of Richmond (1). No doubt Elizabeth Woodville, once convinced that her sons were no more, hoped to gain considerable influence for herself by means of Henry's projected marriage to her daughter; presumably Margaret Beaufort Countess of Richmond (Henry Tudor's mother) and John Morton Bishop of Ely had similar aspirations. Perhaps, as Sir Thomas More suggests, it was Morton (held in captivity by the duke) who persuaded Buckingham to become involved (4): certainly, it is difficult to see why a man who, thanks in part to Richard III's patronage, had become second only to the king in power in the realm should have rebelled at all unless out of sheer greed and the anticipation of even greater gains (3, 4). Recently, historians have been inclined to play down the importance of the Duke of Buckingham altogether: it has even been suggested, indeed, that he only joined in after the rebellion in Wales (initially directed against both Richard III and himself) was already underway, and that his participation at a late stage in fact helps explain its failure. Lack of coordination between the various strands of unrest, and poor organization generally, was certainly a major factor too, as was the king's own vigorous and effective response to the challenge. Moreover, much of the country (particularly the north of England) remained loyal to Richard III. The Kentish rebels rose prematurely, it seems, and were firmly crushed by John Howard Duke of Norfolk (5). News of armed moves against him, including the involvement of the Duke of Buckingham, had reached the king at Lincoln by 11 October when he wrote requesting assistance from the city of York (6); while both Richard's anger at Buckingham's treachery and his determination to resist insurrection are clearly evident in a letter to the chancellor penned the following day (7) and a series of entries on the *Patent Rolls* (9). Chronicles tended to dwell particularly on the failure of the Welsh revolt, the ignominious betrayal of Buckingham, and his peremptory execution at Salisbury on 2 November 1483 (1, 2, 3). Yet it was in southern England where the real danger lay: here Henry Tudor came within an ace of landing and, had he made it in time, he might well have found enough support to mount a potentially fatal challenge to Richard III. It is certainly significant that the Yorkist king *himself* took charge of the counter-offensive in the south-west (1, 3, 9).

Clearly, the October rebellion was on a considerable scale and, although both Buckingham's failure in Wales and the rapid reactions of the king are notable, many southerners had firmly committed themselves to the Tudor rose. Indeed, as Rosemary Horrox has convincingly argued, Buckingham's rebellion was not only a profound shock to the king and a severe blow to his self-confidence but it was to help shape royal policy for the rest of the reign. Since it marked Richard's failure to take over Edward IV's power structure and resulted in the emergence of Henry Tudor as an acknowledged alternative to the Yorkist dynasty, in fact, he now faced the awesome task of reconstructing political control over most of southern and western England virtually from scratch. Moreover, he probably had little choice, given the extent of southern defection and the number of former Edwardian loyalists who now fled the country, but to promote many members of *his* former ducal affinity, particularly northerners, in the rebellion's aftermath—even though such a policy was always liable to raise as many problems as it solved.

1) Crowland Chronicle
(*Crowland*, pp. 163, 165, 169)

In order to release [Edward V and his brother] from captivity the people of the South and West of the kingdom began to murmur greatly, to form assemblies and to organise associations to this end...

When at last the people round the city of London and in Kent, Essex, Sussex, Hampshire, Dorset, Devon, Somerset, Wiltshire and Berkshire and also in some other southern counties of the kingdom ... began considering vengeance, public proclamation having been made that Henry Duke of Buckingham, then living at Brecknock in Wales, being repentant of what had been done would be captain-in-chief in this affair, a rumour arose that King Edward's sons, by some unknown manner of violent destruction, had met their fate. For this reason, all those who had begun this agitation, realising that if they could not find someone new at their head for their conquest it would soon be all over with them, remembered Henry Earl of Richmond, who had already spent many years in exile in Brittany. A message was sent to him by the Duke of Buckingham on the advice of the lord Bishop of Ely, his prisoner at Brecknock, inviting him to hasten into the kingdom of England as fast as he could reach the shore to marry Elizabeth, the dead king's elder daughter, and with her, at the same time, take possession of the whole kingdom.

This whole conspiracy was known well enough, through spies, to King Richard who never acted sleepily but incisively and with the utmost vigilance, and he arranged that in Wales as well as in all parts of the Marches there, round about the duke, armed men should be held in readiness to pounce on all his domestic possessions as soon as the duke moved a foot away from his house and who, encouraged by the duke's great wealth which the king had transferred to them for that reason, would hinder his crossing in every way. And so it was done; for on that side of the castle of Brecknock which faces the interior of Wales, Thomas, son of the deceased Sir Roger Vaughan, in association with his brothers and kinsmen, kept a most diligent watch over all the surrounding countryside, while Humphrey Stafford destroyed part of the bridges and ferries which crossed into England and closed the other part by bringing up strong guards.

The duke, meanwhile, was staying at Weobley, the home of Walter Devereux Lord Ferrers, together with the Bishop of Ely and his other advisers. Realising that he was hemmed in and could find no safe way out, he secretly changed his attire and forsook his men; he was finally discovered in the cottage of a certain poor man because the supply of provisions there was greater than usual; he was seized and taken to the city of Salisbury where the king had arrived with a great army and he suffered capital punishment in the public market-place of that city [on 2 November].

On the following day the king proceeded with the whole army towards the western parts of the kingdom, where all his enemies had taken up their position except those from Kent who were at Guildford awaiting the outcome of the affair, and reached the city of Exeter. Overcome by fear at this terrible arrival Peter Courtenay Bishop of Exeter, as well as Thomas Marquis of Dorset and various other nobles of neighbouring districts who had conspired in the rebellion, or as many of them as could find ships in readiness, took to the sea and finally landed on the desired shores of Brittany. Others lay low for a time in hiding-places under the shelter of friends and afterwards entrusted themselves to the protection of holy places...

[While] the king was still in the city of Exeter, Henry Earl of Richmond, unaware of these disturbances, with certain ships, placed himself and the men with whom he had sailed from Brittany below the mouth of Plymouth harbour in order to investigate the state of affairs. At length he was informed how matters stood concerning both the death of the Duke of Buckingham and the flight of his own supporters and, hoisting his sails, he put to sea again.

2) Vitellius AXVI
(*Vitellius AXVI*, pp. 191-2)

... many knights and gentlemen, of Kent and other places, gathered them together to have gone towards the Duke of Buckingham, being then at Brecknock in the march of Wales, which intended to have subdued King Richard; for anon as King Richard had put to death the lord chamberlain and other gentlemen ... he also put to death the children of King Edward, for which cause he lost the hearts of the people. And thereupon many gentlemen intended his destruction. And when the king knew of the duke's intent, anon he went westward; and there raised his people, whereof the duke feared and fled, because at that time his people were not come to him; and so departed from his manor of Brecknock in secret wise unto a servant's place of his, named Bannister, where he was a while. Then King Richard made proclamation... that whatever man might take the duke should have £1000 in money and £100 of land.... Then this Bannister, hearing that proclamation, what for the lucre of these goods on the one part and fear for his life and goods on the other, if he had been disclosed by any other person than himself... caused the sheriff [to] take him in the same Bannister's place. And so [he was] brought to the king at Salisbury; where, the second day after his coming, without speaking with King Richard, [he was] beheaded...

Then the gentlemen who had intended to have gone to him, hearing of his taking, fled sore dismayed; for at this time, when the duke took contrary part against King Richard, the greater part of the gentlemen of England were so dismayed that they knew not whose part to take.... And upon the beheading of the duke, King Richard rode to Exeter...

3) Polydore Vergil
(*Vergil*, pp. 192, 193, 194, 195, 197, 198, 199, 200, 201, 202, 204)

... a conspiracy was contrived against [the king] by means of Henry Duke of Buckingham which, though it was by one of the conspirators disclosed before it grew great, yet was he troubled in suppressing thereof...

[The duke] demanded of King Richard that part of the Earl of Hereford's patrimony that to him by right of inheritance was due. To this King Richard... is reported to have answered forthwith in great rage... [The King's] answer settled deep into the duke's breast who, from that time forth, moved much with ire and indignation, began to devise by what means he might thrust out that ungrateful man from the royal seat for whose cause he had right often done many things against his own conscience.... And so he began to disclose his intent to John Bishop of Ely... showing how he had devised the means whereby both the blood of King Edward and of Henry the Sixth that yet was remaining, being conjoined by affinity, might be restored to the dominion due unto both their progenies. The means was this, that Henry Earl of Richmond... might be sent for in all haste possible, and assisted with all that they might do, so that he would promise... that after he had once obtained the kingdom he would take to wife Elizabeth, King Edward's daughter...

[At] the very same time a plot of new conspiracy was laid in London between Elizabeth the queen, wife to King Edward, and Margaret mother to Earl Henry [concerning the] conjoining of both the houses... Henry having received the message gave thanks to God [and] gave notice of his coming...

While these things were adoing, King Richard was informed of the conspiracy of these noble men...

[The duke] made ready for war, and persuaded his confederates... to raise the people. So almost at one moment and time Thomas Marquis Dorset, Edward Courtenay, with Peter his brother, Bishop of Exeter in Devonshire, Richard Guildford, with certain of great reputation, in Kent, raised up the commons everywhere to armour, and made a beginning of wars. But King Richard the same season having gathered a huge host of armed men... resolved to... turn his whole army against the head, that was the duke, who removing from London took his journey towards Salisbury.... And now was he come within two days' journey of the town, when the duke, with great force of Welsh soldiers, whom he, as a sore and hard dealing man, had brought to the field against their wills, and without any lust to fight for him, rather by rigorous commandment than for money, which was the cause of the revolt, went earnestly about to encounter the king, but he was forsaken suddenly by the greater part of his soldiers, and compelled thereby to fly ... into the house of a certain servant of his named Humphrey Bannister.... When his confederates, who had now begun war, knew that the duke was forsaken by his people, and fled no man knew whither, they were suddenly dismayed, every man fled without hope of safety, and others, got into sanctuaries or wilderness, or determined to sail overseas, whereof a great part came safely soon after into Brittany. Amongst that company was Peter Courtenay Bishop of Exeter, with Edward his brother, Earl of Devonshire, Thomas Marquis Dorset, Edward Woodville, a valiant man of war, brother to Queen Elizabeth.... Also John Morton Bishop of Ely, with many other noble men, transported over about the same time into Flanders...

[Humphrey] Bannister, whether for fear or money there is some doubt, betrayed his guest Henry the duke and brought him forthwith to Salisbury unto King Richard. The duke was diligently examined, and what he knew upon demand he told without torture, hoping because he freely confessed, that therefore he should have liberty to speak with Richard, which he most sore desired; but after he had confessed the offence he was beheaded...

While these things were done in England, Henry Earl of Richmond had prepared an army of 5000 Bretons, and furnished a navy of 15 ships, [and] begun to sail with a prosperous wind... [But] Earl Henry, viewing afar off all the shore beset with soldiers which King Richard had everywhere disposed, [and seeing] none of his own ships within view, hoisted up sail and with prosperous wind came into Normandy...

[King] Richard, being returned to London, commanded certain that were guilty of the conspiracy, who were taken in sundry places, [even men] of his own household, to be put to death.

4) Sir Thomas More
(*More*, pp. 87-90)

... soon after began the conspiracy or rather good confederation between the Duke of Buckingham and many other gentlemen against [the king]. The occasion whereupon the king and the duke fell out is, by diverse folk, diverse ways asserted...

[After Richard III's coronation he and the duke] parted, as it seemed, very great friends, at Gloucester. From whence, as soon as the duke came home, he so lightly turned from him and so highly conspired against him that a man would marvel whereof the change grew.... Some have I heard say that the duke, a little before the coronation, among other things required of the protector the Duke of Hereford's lands, to which he pretended himself just inheritor ...

[But Richard] rejected the duke's request with many spiteful and threatening words; which so wounded his heart with hatred and mistrust that he never after could endure to look right at King Richard but ever feared for his own life... [Yet] many right wise men think it unlikely—the deep dissimulating nature of both these men considered, and what need in that green world the protector had of the duke, and in what peril the duke stood if he fell once under the suspicion of the tyrant—that either the protector would give the duke occasion of displeasure or the duke the protector occasion of mistrust.... Very truth it is, the duke was a proud-minded man, and evilly could bear the glory of another, so that I have heard of some that said they saw it, that the duke at such time as the crown was first set upon the protector's head, his eye could not abide the sight thereof... [And] soon after his coming home to Brecknock, having there in his custody [the] Bishop of Ely, [he] waxed with him familiar; whose wisdom abused his pride, to his own deliverance and the duke's destruction.

5) Paston Letters, John Duke of Norfolk to John Paston, 10 October 1483
(*Paston Letters,* Vol. 6, p. 73)

... it is so that the Kentishmen be up in the Weald, and say that they will come and rob the city [of London], which I shall prevent if I may. Therefore I pray you that with all diligence you make you ready and come hither [to London], and bring with you six tall fellows in harness...

6) York Civic Records, Richard III, in Lincoln, to the city of York, 11 October 1483
(*York Civic Records,* Vol. 1, pp. 83-4)

... the Duke of Buckingham is traitorously turned upon us contrary to the duty of his allegiance, and intends the utter destruction of us, you all, and all other our true subjects that have taken our part, whose traitorous intent we with God's grace intend briefly to resist and subdue. We desire and pray you [that] you will send unto us as many men defensibly arrayed on horseback as you may goodly make to our town of Leicester, the 21st day of this present month, without fail...

7) Richard III to the chancellor, 12 October 1483
(Hammond and Sutton, *Richard III: The Road to Bosworth Field*, pp. 144-5)

... we by God's grace intend briefly to advance us towards our rebel and traitor the Duke of Buckingham to resist and withstand his malicious purpose.... For which cause it behoves us to have our great seal here...

Here [at Lincoln], loved be God, is all well and truly determined, and for to resist the malice of him that had best cause to be true, the Duke of Buckingham, the most untrue creature living; whom with God's grace we shall not be long till we will be in those parts and subdue his malice. We assure you [that] never was false traitor better provided for...

8) Plumpton Correspondence, Edward Plumpton to Sir Robert Plumpton, 18 October 1483
(*Plumpton Correspondence*, pp. 44-5)

People in this country [Lancashire] be so troubled, in such commandment as they have in the king's name and otherwise, marvellously, that they know not what to do. My Lord Strange goes forth from Lathum upon Monday next with 10,000 men, whither we cannot say. The Duke of Buckingham has so many men, as it is said here, that he is able to go where he will; but I trust he shall be right withstood and all his malice; and else were great pity. Messengers come daily, both from the king's grace and the duke, into this country.

9) Chancery Patent Rolls
(*CPR, 1476–85*, pp. 370-1)

a) *23 October 1483* (Leicester): general commission of array to Francis Viscount Lovell, the king's chamberlain, for the resistance of the rebel Henry Duke of Buckingham.

b) *23 October 1483* (Leicester): precept to the sheriffs of Devon, Cornwall, Salop, Wiltshire etc. to issue a proclamation denouncing Thomas, late Marquis of Dorset, and also denouncing several individuals who have assembled the people by the comfort of the great rebel the late Duke of Buckingham and the Bishops of Ely and Salisbury, and offering rewards for their capture and pardon for all who withdrew from them.

c) *5 November 1483* (Bridport): commission of array in Wales to William Earl of Huntingdon and Sir James Tyrell for the resistance of the rebels.

d) *8 November 1483* (Exeter): commission to Thomas Earl of Surrey (and others) to summon men of the counties of Kent and Sussex to besiege the castle of Bodiam, co. Sussex, which the rebels have seized.

e) *13 November 1483* (Exeter): commission of array in the counties of Devon and Cornwall to John Lord Scrope of Bolton for the resistance of the rebels.

f) *13 November 1483* (Exeter): commissions issued to arrest and imprison rebels in Devon, Cornwall, Somerset, Dorset, Southampton, Wiltshire, Oxford and Berkshire.

11

POLITICS, PATRONAGE AND GOVERNMENT DURING THE REIGN OF RICHARD III

Richard III's most pressing problem, in the months following Buckingham's rebellion, was not only to plug gaps in the royal household, central government and local administration occasioned by the defections of October 1483 but also to take steps to ensure that, never again, could his power and authority as England's king be challenged as it had been by so many Edwardian loyalists. Clearly, if this was to be accomplished successfully, it was crucially important that he use the patronage at his disposal (greatly enhanced by attainders and forfeitures in the parliament of January 1484) to best effect in securing his regime and, as both the *Patent Rolls* and *Harleian Manuscript 433* demonstrate, he did indeed distribute largesse on an impressive scale (7a, b). Many nobility and gentry benefited, including John Howard Duke of Norfolk and his son Thomas Howard Earl of Surrey, the king's nephew John de la Pole Earl of Lincoln, William Herbert Earl of Huntingdon, John Lord Dinham, Francis Viscount Lovell and William Catesby. Nor were men from southern and western counties excluded, providing they had remained loyal to the king (whether by political inclination, perceived self-interest, sound judgement or sheer good fortune) during the recent upheavals. Nevertheless, what is most striking about Richard III's political patronage post-October 1483 is the advancement of northerners, many of them from families associated with Richard of Gloucester during the 1470s and early 1480s (7a, b).

Most northerners remained firmly stationed in their native counties, ensuring continuity of service there, although often attracting new fees, lands and responsibilities. What made the second Crowland continuator wring his clerical hands in despair, however, was the plantation of northerners south of Trent, particularly, as the records show, in south-eastern, central-southern and south-western England (where they might be blatant newcomers, often displacing long-established local families in their own accustomed spheres of influence): indeed, according to the chronicler, such was their impact that southerners 'murmured ceaselessly and longed more each day for the return of their old lords in place of the tyranny of the present ones' (1). Certainly, such men *can* be found holding important offices and receiving grants of estates not only in southern counties but in the midlands too, as well as obtaining advancement in the royal household and central administration. Moreover, although their numbers were not so large as to swamp either the king's household or local government, their pivotal position in Richard III's regime in 1484–5 cannot seriously be doubted: even if the king regarded the plantation of northerners in the south as only a temporary expedient to counter recent disloyalty, they frequently occupied posts of vital importance in preventing future rebellion and defending the south coast against possible invasion, as well as providing a formidable cohort of knights and esquires of the body around his person. Since hostility to Richard in the home counties and southern England continued to simmer, however, the wisdom of such a policy is questionable and, indeed, has a real ring of desperation to it. Not all northerners proved loyal to the king, moreover, when it came to the crunch at Bosworth: Henry Percy Earl of Northumberland, Thomas Lord Stanley and Sir William Stanley, in particular, despite benefiting significantly from royal patronage, failed him in the end. If we can believe the *Ballad of Bosworth Field* (a controversial source, dismissed by Colin Richmond for one as both late and desperately unreliable), many more came up trumps and at least set out for Bosworth (7c)—even if they did not arrive in time for the battle, not fight very hard if they did make it, or not engage Henry Tudor's invading force at all!

Since he reigned for so short a time, it is difficult to judge Richard III's potential and qualities as a ruler or draw meaningful conclusions about his government as king; also, what looks like good kingship and firm government may, in reality, be nothing more than Richard trying to widen and deepen his basis of support. Nevertheless, he does seem to compare not unfavourably with Edward IV and Henry VII (neither of whom, incidentally, would have much of a reputation if they had to be assessed merely on their early years in power): indeed, if we are to believe the *Rous Roll*, Richard III ruled his subjects 'full commendably, punishing offenders of his laws, especially extortioners and oppressors of his commons' and won the 'love of all his subjects rich and poor'. Ricardians certainly draw attention to the statutes passed by the king's only parliament and with some justification: even if he was primarily concerned to enhance his popularity, he did sanction (and perhaps encourage) measures—such as the act condemning benevolences (8b)—which clearly benefited his people. Beneficial to poorer men and women in particular (and Richard does seem to have had a genuine compassion for them) was his designation of John Harrington as clerk of the council of requests and supplications in December 1483 (8a), a judicial offshoot of the king's council designed to make royal justice more accessible. Richard's continued interest in the government of the north, and determination to maintain his authority there (even, if necessary, at the expense of border magnates such as Henry Percy

Earl of Northumberland), is demonstrated by his retaining the wardenship of the west marches in his own hands (with the lesser northern peer Humphrey Lord Dacre of Gilsland as deputy) and his establishment of the popular (and enduring) Council of the North in July 1484 under the control of his nephew John de la Pole Earl of Lincoln (7a, 8c). The king certainly identified himself strongly, too, with promoting justice and securing law and order in the provinces, as is evident from documents such as the royal proclamation in Kent following Buckingham's rebellion and the interesting instructions to Sir Marmaduke Constable as steward of Tutbury (8c), even if his success was only limited. Chronicles tend to be critical of Richard III's financial demands once he had, in their view, dissipated the wealth inherited from Edward IV (1, 3, 4): in fact, far from bequeathing a vast fortune, his brother's treasury was almost empty at his death; Richard did make efforts to improve royal financial administration (8c); and the need to provide for defence against an anticipated invasion by Henry Tudor in 1484-5 did not come cheap, even forcing the king to raise an unpopular national loan in the spring of 1485 (1).

Real or imagined threats to his throne, and genuine fear for the succession following the death of his only legitimate son in April 1484 (1, 2), dominate much of Richard III's reign. Concern to neutralize continuing Woodville discontent probably helps explain his provision for Elizabeth Woodville and her daughters early in 1484 (1, 5); the king's nervousness later in the year no doubt lay behind the firm measures against William Collingbourne and John Turberville (3); and his continued determination both to ruin Henry Tudor's plans and provide for the succession (despite having designated his nephew the Earl of Lincoln as heir) probably explains his reported ambition to marry his own niece Elizabeth of York early in 1485. Inevitably, Queen Anne's death in March 1485 gave rise to rumours that she had been poisoned (2, 4), and, whatever his intentions may or may not have been, Richard III had no choice but to deny any marital designs on his niece (1, 6). Northern resistance to the project may well have been crucial here (1), for, despite all his recent efforts to widen the basis of his political support, the king still remained dangerously dependent on his northern connection: indeed, this ill-fated scheme, far from consolidating his position, may have proved counter-productive in the end since it perhaps weakened his northern support and helped determine the outcome of Bosworth.

1) Crowland Chronicle
(*Crowland*, pp. 169, 171, 173, 175, 177, 183)

[Following the defeat of Buckingham's rebellion] the king gradually reduced his army, dismissing those who had been summoned for the expedition from the far marches of the North, and came to London triumphant over the enemy without a battle but at no less expense than if the armies had fought hand to hand. So began the rapid consumption of that very rich treasure which King Edward thought he had left behind him for very different and long-term purposes...

Parliament began about 22 January [1484]. In that assembly the title by which the king, in the previous summer, had ascended to the height of the crown was corroborated; even though that lay court was not empowered to determine on it since there was a dispute concerning the validity of a marriage, nevertheless it presumed to do so on account of the great fear affecting the most steadfast. Besides and beyond this, so many great lords, nobles, magnates and commoners, and even three bishops, were attainted that we nowhere read of the like even under the triumvirate of Octavian, Anthony and Lepidus. What great numbers and inheritances were amassed in the king's treasury in consequence! He distributed all these amongst his northerners whom he had planted in every part of his dominions, to the shame of all the southern people who murmured ceaselessly and longed more each day for the return of their old lords in place of the tyranny of the present ones.

While the supreme council of the kingdom was in session and after Queen Elizabeth, urged by frequent intercessions and dire threats, had sent all her daughters out of the sanctuary at Westminster to King Richard, it happened one February afternoon that, by special command of the king, there were gathered together... almost all the lords spiritual and temporal and the leading knights and gentlemen of the king's household, the chief of whom seemed to be John Howard, whom the king had recently created Duke of Norfolk. Each person subscribed his name to a certain new oath... undertaking to adhere to the king's only son, Edward, as their supreme lord, should anything happen to his father.

Shortly afterwards, however, they learned how vain are the attempts of man to regulate his affairs without God. In the following April... this only son, on whom, through so many solemn oaths, all hopes of the royal succession rested, died in Middleham castle after a short illness.... You might have seen the father and mother, after hearing the news at Nottingham, where they were then staying, almost out of their minds for a long time with the sudden grief...

[At the beginning of 1485] he reckoned, astutely, that money, already beginning to run very short, was the sinews of war and resorted to the exactions of King Edward which he himself had condemned in Parliament, only avoiding in every case the word 'benevolence'. Selected men were sent out... who extorted great sums of money from the coffers of persons of almost every rank in the kingdom, by prayers or threats, by fair means or foul...

[Already by Christmas 1484] it was said by many that the king was applying his mind in every way to contracting a marriage with [his niece] Elizabeth, either after the death of the queen or by means of a divorce for which he believed he had sufficient grounds. He saw no other way of confirming his crown and dispelling the hopes of his rival. A few days later the queen began to be seriously ill and her sickness was then believed to have got worse and worse because the king himself was completely spurning his consort's bed. Therefore he judged it right to consult with doctors.... About the middle of the following March (1485)... Queen Anne died and was buried at Westminster...

Eventually the king's plan and his intention to marry Elizabeth, his close blood-relation, was related to some who were opposed to it and, after the council had been summoned, the king was compelled to make his excuses at length, saying that such a thing had never entered his mind. There were some at that council who knew well enough that the contrary was true. Those who were most strongly against this marriage and whose wills the king scarcely ever dared to oppose were in fact Sir Richard Ratcliffe and William Catesby, squire of the body. These men told the king, to his face, that if he did not deny any such purpose and did not counter it by public declaration before the mayor and commonalty of the city of London, the northerners, in whom he placed the greatest trust, would all rise against him, charging him with causing the death of the queen... in order to complete his incestuous association with his near kinswoman, to the offence of God. In addition they brought in over a dozen doctors of theology who asserted that the Pope had no power of dispensation over that degree of consanguinity. It was thought by many that these men and others like them put so many obstacles in the way through fear that if Elizabeth attained the rank and dignity of queen it might be in her power, sometime, to avenge the death of her uncle Earl Anthony and her brother Richard, upon those who had been the principal counsellors in the affair. Shortly before Easter, therefore, the king... in the presence of the mayor and citizens of London, in a clear loud voice, carried out fully the advice to make a denial of this kind—as many people believed, more by the will of these counsellors than his own.

King Richard... and many others were killed in that frenzy of battle [at Bosworth]; and many northerners in whom, especially, Richard placed so much trust, fled even before coming to blows with the enemy.

2) John Rous
(Hanham, *Richard III and his Early Historians 1483–1535*, pp. 121, 122-3)

This King Richard was praiseworthy for his building, as at Westminster, Nottingham, Warwick, York and Middleham, and many other places, which can be viewed. He founded a noble chantry for a hundred priests in the cathedral of York, and another college at Middleham. He founded another in the church of St Mary of Barking, by the Tower of London, and endowed the Queen's College at Cambridge with 500 marks of annual rent. The money which was offered him by the peoples of London, Gloucester and Worcester he declined with thanks, affirming that he would rather have their love than their treasure...

[Following Buckingham's rebellion] many lords fled from the country, and shortly after the prince [of Wales] died a tragic death at Easter-tide.... Not long after... the young Earl of Warwick, Edward, eldest son of George Duke of Clarence, was proclaimed heir apparent in the royal court.... Later he was placed in custody and the Earl of Lincoln was preferred to him...

And Lady Anne [Richard III's] queen, daughter of the Earl of Warwick, [the king] poisoned.

3) Fabian's Chronicle
(*Fabian*, pp. 671-2)

King Richard [in 1484/5], leading his life in great agony and doubt, trusting few of those about him, spared not to spend the great treasure which King Edward IV had gathered in giving great and large gifts; by means whereof he not only wasted the great treasure of his brother but also was in such great danger that he borrowed many notable sums of money from rich men of this realm, and especially from the citizens of London, whereof the least sum was £40, for surety whereof he delivered to them good and sufficient pledges.

During this time many gentlemen... departed over the sea into France and there allied themselves with the virtuous Prince Henry, son unto the Earl of Richmond ... [Of] that affinity one, named William Collingbourne, was taken and, after he had been held a season in prison, he, with another gentlemen named Turberville, was brought to the Guildhall and arraigned. While Turberville was reprieved to prison, the other was cast for sundry treasons and for a rhyme [in] derision of the king and his council, as follows:

> The cat, the rat, and Lovell our dog
> Ruleth all England under a hog.

By which was meant that Catesby, Ratcliffe and Lord Lovell ruled the land under the king who bore the white boar.... For this and other [offences] he was put to the most cruel death on Tower Hill where, for him, was made a new pair of gallows upon which, after he had hanged a short season, he was cut down, being alive, and his bowels ripped out of his belly and cast into the fire there by him, and lived till the butcher put his hand into the bulk of his body; insomuch that he said in the same instant, 'O Lord Jesu, yet more trouble', and so died to the great compassion of many people.

4) Polydore Vergil
(*Vergil*, pp. 191-2, 204, 211, 212)

... because he could not reform the thing that was past, [Richard] determined to abolish by all dutifulness the note of infamy with which his honour was stained, and to give such hope of his good government that from thenceforth no man should be able to lay any calamity that might happen to the commonwealth to his charge.... And so, whether it were for that cause or... because he now repented of his evil deeds, he began... to give the show and countenance of a good man, whereby he might be accounted more righteous, more mild, better affected to the commonalty, and more liberal especially towards the poor; and so first might merit pardon for his offences at God's hand; then after appease partly the envy of man, and procure him goodwill, he began many works as well public as private.... He founded a college at York of a hundred priests. Also he began now to give ear to the good admonition of his friends. But anon after it appeared evident that fear... made King Richard so suddenly good, forasmuch as the bountifulness of the man, being but counterfeit, waxed cold again quickly; by reason whereof all his proposed practices began straightway to come to nought. For first he lost Edward his only son the third month after he had been made Prince of Wales; after that a conspiracy was contrived by means of Henry Duke of Buckingham...

Afterward he assembled a parliament, wherein he procured all the exiles to be denounced as traitors to their country by act of parliament; then all their goods to be confiscated; and not content with that, though very rich, he finally caused a great tax of money to be imposed upon the people, for he had of late been so lavish in rewards, seeking by such means to purge himself, and win favour of the commonalty, that he began now to be needy...

[The] queen, whether she were despatched with sorrowfulness, or poison, died.... The king, thus loosed from the bond of matrimony, began to cast an eye upon Elizabeth his niece, and to desire her in marriage; but both because the young lady herself, and all others, did abhor the wickedness so detestable, he determined therefore to do everything by leisure, forasmuch as he was overwhelmed with pinching cares on every hand; for that some men of name passed over daily unto Henry, others favoured secretly the partners of conspiracy...

5) Richard III's oath to provide for Elizabeth Woodville and her daughters, 1 March 1484
(Hammond and Sutton, *Richard III: The Road to Bosworth Field*, pp. 165-6)

I, Richard... promise and swear... that if the daughters of Elizabeth Grey, late calling herself queen of England... will come to me out of the sanctuary of Westminster... then I shall see that they shall be in surety of their lives [and] have all things requisite and necessary for their exhibition and finding as my kinswomen. And that I shall marry such of them as now be marriageable to gentlemen born, and give each of them marriage lands etc. to the yearly value of 200 marks.... And over this that I shall yearly [pay] for the exhibition and finding of Elizabeth Grey... the sum of 700 marks.... And moreover I promise them that if any surmise or evil report be made to me of them ... by any person... then I shall not give thereunto faith nor credence...

6) Mercers' Company Records, 1485
(*English Historical Documents 1327–1485*, ed. A. R. Myers, p. 342)

... as there have been long discussions and much uninformed talk among the people by evil-disposed persons, who have... sown these rumours to the very great displeasure of the king, showing how the queen was poisoned by consent and will of the king, so that he might marry and have to wife the Lady Elizabeth, eldest daughter of his brother, late king of England ... the king sent for and had before him [the] mayor and aldermen. And in the great hall, in the presence of many of his lords and many other people, he showed his grief and displeasure, and said it never came into his thought or mind to marry in such manner, nor was he pleased or glad at the death of his queen but as sorry and as heavy in heart as a man would be...

7) Political Patronage of Richard III: a selection of evidence showing northerners in Richard III's service and their advancement

a) *Chancery Patent Rolls*

(CPR, 1476–85, pp. 367, 409, 462, 464, 388, 485-6, 502, 368, 579, 563, 392, 380, 482, 397, 398, 490, 579, 563, 393, 387, 399, 398, 492, 563, 392, 398, 400, 471, 557, 490, 491, 410, 572, 399, 557, 393, 415, 437, 436, 400-1, 490-1)

Henry Percy Earl of Northumberland
November 1483: great chamberlain of England
February 1484: for his good service in the attainment of the king's right and crown, and in defence of the realm towards Scotland, with Alan Percy his son, the manor and lordship of Holderness in Yorkshire
July 1484: warden of the east and middle marches towards Scotland September 1484: captain of the town and castle of Berwick

Humphrey Lord Dacre of Gilsland
March 1484: annuity of 100 marks *September 1484*: king's councillor, warden of the west march towards Scotland

John Lord Scrope of Bolton
December 1484: king's councillor, for his good services against the rebels, manors in Cornwall, Devon and Somerset, worth in excess of £200 yearly
December 1484: king's councillor, constable of Exeter and steward of all lordships and lands pertaining to it, with an annuity of 200 marks

Thomas Lord Stanley
November 1483: king's councillor, constable of England
September 1484: with his son George Stanley Lord Strange, for their good service against the rebels, castles, manors, lordships etc. in Cheshire, Somerset, Wiltshire, Berkshire, Bedfordshire, Hertfordshire, Huntingdonshire, Lancashire and the city of London, to the yearly value of 1000 marks

Sir William Stanley
November 1483: knight of the body, chief justice of North Wales

Sir Ralph Ashton of Fritton-in-Redesdale, Yorkshire and Middleton, Lancashire
October 1483: vice-constable of England to proceed against persons guilty of lese majesté
December 1483: J.P., North Riding of Yorkshire and Kent; commissioner to enquire into treasons etc. in Kent
March 1484: knight of the body, tun of wine yearly
May 1484: king's servant, knight of the body, for his good service against the rebels, manors, lands etc. in Kent, worth in excess of £110; lieutenant to the Earl of Arundel as constable of Dover castle and warden of the cinque ports; commissioner of array, Kent
December 1484: commissioner of array, Kent

Sir Ralph Bigod of Settrington, Yorkshire
December 1483: J.P., East Riding of Yorkshire and Kent; commissioner to enquire into treasons etc. in Yorkshire
March 1484: knight of the body, master of the king's ordnance
May 1484: commissioner of array, East Riding of Yorkshire and Kent
   December 1484: commissioner of array, East Riding of Yorkshire

Sir Marmaduke Constable of Flamborough, Yorkshire
December 1483: J.P., Kent; commissioner to enquire into treasons etc. in
    Kent
May 1484: commissioner of array, Kent and Derbyshire
September 1484: king's servant, for his good service against the rebels, the
    manors of Bosworth and Braunston, Leicestershire
December 1484: J.P., Derbyshire; commissioner of array, Derbyshire and
    Staffordshire

Sir John Saville of Thornhill, Yorkshire
February 1484: lieutenant or captain of the Isle of Wight
March 1484: J.P., Southampton
May 1484: commissioner of array, Southampton

Sir Thomas Wortley of Wortley, Yorkshire
December 1483: J.P., Derbyshire, commissioner to enquire into treasons etc.
    in Derbyshire and Nottinghamshire
March 1484: for his good service against the rebels, manors etc. in Staffordshire
    and Kent; constable of Stafford castle and steward of Buckingham
    lordships in Staffordshire; steward of the lordship of Scarsdale and town of
    Chesterfield, Derbyshire
May/December 1484: commissioner of array, Derbyshire and Staffordshire

b) *Harleian Manuscript 433*
(*Harleian MS 433*, Vol. 2, pp. 39-40, 136, Vol. 1, p. 74, Vol. 3, p. 124, Vol. 1,
    p. 100, Vol. 2, pp. 61-2, 189, Vol. 1, pp. 117, 126, 138, 100, 102, Vol. 2, pp.
    60, 76, Vol. 1, pp. 174, 238, Vol. 2, p. 44, Vol. 1, p. 282)

Henry Percy Earl of Northumberland
December 1483: authority to take possession of castles, manors, lordships etc.
    in Kent, Essex, Devon, Gloucestershire, Dorset, Somerset, Suffolk, Surrey
    and Pembrokeshire

Humphrey Lord Dacre
June 1484: lieutenant of Carlisle

John Lord Scrope of Bolton
1483/4: chamberlain of the duchy of Lancaster
April 1484: steward of the temporalities of the bishopric of Exeter

Thomas Lord Stanley

1483/4: annuity of £100 December 1483: authority to seize manors, lordships etc. in Lancashire, Cheshire, Wiltshire, Warwickshire, Leicestershire, Bedfordshire, Somerset, Hertfordshire, Rutland, Oxfordshire and Wales, late of Sir Thomas St Leger, Thomas Marquis of Dorset and Henry Duke of Buckingham, rebels

January 1485: deputed, with Lord Strange and Sir William Stanley, to have the rule and keeping of all persons appointed to do the king's service in the county of Chester when they be warned against the king's rebels; similarly, in the county of Lancaster.

Sir William Stanley

1483/4: chamberlain and sheriff of the counties of Chester and Flint; annuity of £20; constable of the castle and captain of the town of Caernarvon, North Wales, with 24 soldiers in his retinue

Sir Ralph Ashton
1483/4: annuity of £20

Sir Ralph Bigod
1483/4: annuity of £40

Sir Marmaduke Constable

December 1483: knight of the body, constable of the castle and steward of the lordship of Tonbridge, and steward of the manors of Penshurst and Brasted, Kent

January 1484: commissioner to take oaths of loyalty in Kent

March 1484: constable of the castle and steward of the honour of Tutbury, master forester of Needwood, and steward of the lordship of Newcastle-under-Lyme, Staffordshire; master forester of Duffield Frith, constable and steward of High Peak, and steward of Ashbourne, Derbyshire; constable of the castle and steward of the lordship of Donington, Leicestershire; annuity of £89/ 16/8d of the revenues of Tutbury.

1484/5: sheriff of Staffordshire

Sir Thomas Wortley

December 1483: knight of the body, sheriff of Staffordshire, authority to take oaths of allegiance in Staffordshire and condemn unlawful liveries

May 1485: lieutenant of Hammes castle for seven years

c) *Ballad of Bosworth Field*
(*Bishop Percy's Folio Manuscript*, ed. J. W. Hales and F. J. Furnivall, Vol. 3, pp. 244-8)

Part of their names you shall hear that came that day to serve their king... the Earl of Northumberland; the Earl of Westmorland; Lord Fitzhugh; Lord Scrope of Upsall; Lord Scrope of Bolton; Lord Dacre, raised all the North country; Lord Lumley; Lord Greystoke, he brought with him a noble company; Sir Henry Percy; Sir Robert Brackenbury; Sir Marmaduke Constable, a noble knight of King Richard's council; Sir William Conyers; Sir John Melton; Sir Robert Ryder, a man of might; Sir Brian Stapleton; Sir Richard Ratcliffe, a noble knight of King Richard's council; Sir Ralph Dacre, out of the North; Sir Christopher Moresby; Sir William Musgrave; Sir Thomas Broughton; Sir William and Sir Richard Tempest; Sir Ralph Ashton; Sir Richard Warde; Sir Robert Middleton; Sir John Neville, of blood so high; Sir James and Sir Robert Harrington; Sir Thomas Pilkington...

[And] all these great oaths swore they that King Richard should keep his crown.

8) The Government of Richard III: evidence from the records

a) *Chancery Patent Rolls*
(*CPR, 1476–85*, p. 413)

27 December 1483: John Harrington, for his good service before the lords and others of the council and elsewhere, and especially in the custody, registration and expedition of bills, requests and supplications of poor persons, granted for life an annuity of £20 at the receipt of the Exchequer, and the office of clerk of the council of requests and supplications.

b) *Statutes of the Realm, 1484*
(*Statutes of the Realm, 1101-1713*, Richard III, chapter 2)

... the king will it to be ordained, by the advice and assent of the lords spiritual and temporal, and the commons, of this present parliament assembled, and by the authority of the same, that his subjects, and the commonalty of this his realm, from henceforth in no wise be charged by no such charge, exaction or imposition, called a benevolence, nor by such like charge; and that no such exactions, called benevolences, before this time taken, be taken... of any of his subjects of this realm hereafter...

c) *Harleian Manuscript 433*
(*Harleian MS 433*, Vol. 2, p. 49, Vol. 3, pp. 107-8, 118, 116-7)

Proclamation in Kent following Buckingham's rebellion

... the king's highness is fully determined to see due administration of justice throughout this his realm... and to reform, punish and subdue all extortions and oppressions in the same. And for the cause wills that, at his coming now into his county of Kent, every person dwelling within the same that finds himself grieved, oppressed or unlawfully wronged make a bill of his complaint and put it to his highness, and he shall be heard and without delay have such convenient remedy as shall accord with his laws. For his grace is utterly determined all his true subjects shall live in rest and quiet and peaceably enjoy their lands, livelihoods and goods according to the laws of this his land...

Council of the North: regulations of July 1484

These articles following be ordained and established by the king's grace to be used and executed by my Lord of Lincoln and the lords and others of his council in the North parts for his surety and the well-being of the inhabitants of the same.

First, the king wills that no lord nor other person appointed to be of his council, for favour, affection, hate, malice or bribery, shall speak in the council otherwise than the king's laws and good conscience shall require, but be indifferent and in no way partial, as far as his wit and reason will allow him, in all manner of matters that shall be administered before them...

[The] council shall meet, wholly if it may be, once in the quarter of the year at least, at York, to hear, examine and order all bills of complaints and others shown there before them, and oftener if the case require.

[The] council shall have authority and power to order and direct [in respect of] all riots, forcible entries, disputes and other misbehaviours against our laws and peace... in these parts...

[Our] council, for great riots... committed in the great lordships or otherwise by any person, shall commit that person to ward in one of our castles near where the riot is committed...

[The] council, as soon as they have knowledge of any assemblies or gatherings made contrary to our laws and peace, [shall arrange] to resist, withstand and punish the same...

[We] will and straitly charge all and each of our officers, true liegemen and subjects in these north parts to be at all times obedient to the commandments of our council in our name, and duly to execute the same, as they and each of them will eschew our great displeasure and indignation...

Memorandum concerning the king's revenues, 1484

A remembrance made, as well for the hasty levy of the king's revenues growing of all his possessions and hereditaments, as for the profitable state and governance of the same.

First, that all the king's officers of his court of Exchequer use and execute hasty process against all manner of persons accountable, and others being the king's debtors, as the case shall require; and also to hear and determine accounts of the same, and the issues, profits and revenues coming thereof to be levied and paid into the king's receipt without delay.

Also that no person accountable, nor other person being in debt to the king, have any respite, postponement or favour in that court, whereby the king's dues may be delayed…. For it has been said that many officers accountable have been receipted of their accounts from year to year, and also by their payments by space of many years, to the king's great hurt, in times past…

Instructions to Sir Marmaduke Constable as steward of the honour of Tutbury

First, that Sir Marmaduke take an oath of all inhabitants in the honour that they shall be true and faithful liegemen to the king, and not be retained to any lord or others, but immediately to the king's grace.

Also, Sir Marmaduke shall see that no liveries nor fees be given within the honour contrary to the law…

Also, where hitherto divers extortions and oppressions have been done by the county bailiffs, the king wills that from henceforth Sir Marmaduke appoint able and well-disposed persons [who are] to be changed from year to year…

12

RICHARD III, FRANCE AND SCOTLAND

When Edward IV died in April 1483, England was at war with Scotland and on the verge of war with France. No doubt Louis XI of France was relieved at Edward's death but, if we are to believe Philippe de Commines (1), he had no sympathy for Richard III's usurpation; nor, following Louis' own demise at the end of August 1483, did the new French regency government (led by Charles VIII's elder sister Anne of Beaujeu) show much inclination to establish more friendly relations. Brittany, Burgundy and Castile, meanwhile, had all been urging Richard to make *war* against France: indeed, according to the English commander in Calais, at the time of Louis XI's death 'the war is open between both nations'. As for Scotland, although a short-lived truce was soon concluded with James III, Richard's intentions, as they had been since at least 1480, remained hostile, even aggressive; moreover, the fact that Alexander Duke of Albany had let an English garrison into Dunbar in April 1483, while the Scottish king was anxious to regain Berwick, hardly made for calm Anglo-Scottish relations, as Thomas Langton Bishop of St David's recognized in September 1483 (4). When, in October 1483, Duke Francis II of Brittany backed Henry Earl of Richmond's abortive invasion of England and continued to provide refuge for Tudor thereafter (1, 2), Richard III reacted by embarking on naval warfare not only against Brittany but France and Scotland as well in the winter of 1483/4: by mid-February 1484, indeed, he was contemplating a full-scale invasion of Scotland (5). Already, in January 1484, the Estates-General had seriously considered the prospect of an English invasion of France, while Charles VIII's minority government was soon urging Duke Francis of Brittany to support another Tudor expedition to England; on 13 March the 'auld' Franco-Scottish alliance against England was renewed; and, at the end of March, Richard III, when writing to Pope Sixtus IV, highlighted 'this most serious war which we are waging with the very cruel and fierce people of the Scots'. Clearly, at this stage, the English king, far from seeking security for his throne by establishing cordial relations with neighbouring powers, was adopting an altogether more high-risk strategy.

Everything changed during the summer and autumn of 1484. News of a possibly imminent invasion by Henry Tudor brought cancellation of the projected English expedition into Scotland but, for several weeks thereafter, Anglo-Scottish relations remained notably turbulent: early in July, indeed, Richard 'had remarkable success against the Scots at sea' while, later in the month, there was a land battle at Lochmaben near Dumfries, perhaps the product of a private initiative by Alexander Duke of Albany, as a result of which 'many English were captured' (3, 7). Letters exchanged between Richard III and James III in late July and early August, however, helped pave the way for a full-scale Anglo-Scottish peace conference at Nottingham in September 1484 (6): Richard himself led the English negotiating team and, although only a three-year truce resulted, it was also agreed that the king's niece Anne de la Pole should marry the son and heir of James III (3, 7). Meanwhile, Richard also embarked on negotiations with Pierre Landais, treasurer of Brittany, clearly aimed at getting his hands on Henry Tudor and finally putting an end to the threat he posed to the Yorkist dynasty. Unfortunately for the English king, Richmond learned of what was afoot and, perhaps only in the nick of time, made a hasty departure from Brittany and sought solace (and support) at the court of Charles VIII instead (1, 2). Inevitably, this had knock-on effects on Anglo-French relations. In the French regency government, Richmond had a potentially far more formidable backer than Francis II of Brittany, and Anne of Beaujeu was unlikely to be fooled if Richard III (who had maintained his naval hostility to France throughout the negotiations with Pierre Landais) now suddenly changed tack and sought her friendship. In fact, he did not: on the contrary, in December 1484, he issued a proclamation condemning Henry Tudor for entering 'the obedience of the king's ancient enemy Charles calling himself King of France' and renewing the English claim to the French throne! During the winter of 1484/5, even if in reality the French government would have struggled to provide any worthwhile backing for Richmond, it probably did not appear so across the English Channel, especially once Tudor made a public appeal for support in France and began mustering modest forces. According to the Crowland chronicler, early in January 1485 Richard III received intelligence that 'without any doubt' his enemies would mount an invasion 'as soon as summer came' (3) and, certainly, by the spring he was raising money and organizing troops to defend his realm. Meanwhile, in France, Charles VIII began to urge backing for Henry Tudor on the grounds that 'he has the most evident right of anyone in the world to the kingdom of England'. The stage was being set, in fact, for what would soon prove the decisive confrontation: the battle of Bosworth on 22 August 1485.

1) Philippe de Commines
(*Commines*, pp. 396, 354-5)

As soon as Edward [IV] was dead our master [Louis XI] was informed. But he showed no signs of joy when he heard it. A few days later he received letters from the Duke of Gloucester. He had had himself made King of England.... King Richard asked for the king's friendship [but] the king did not reply to his letters nor listen to his envoys and he considered him extremely cruel and evil...

God raised up an enemy against him [Richard III] who had no power. This was the Earl of Richmond, at that time a prisoner in Brittany, today King of England. He was a member of the house of Lancaster but he was not the closest claimant to the crown.... He himself told me on one occasion, a short while before he left this kingdom, that since the age of five he had been guarded like a fugitive or kept in prison. For fifteen years or thereabouts this Earl of Richmond had been held prisoner in Brittany by Duke Francis.... He had fallen into his hands during a storm when he was attempting to flee to France with his uncle [Jasper Tudor] Earl of Pembroke [in 1471]. I was at the duke's court at the time they were captured. The duke treated them very gently as prisoners and on the death of King Edward, the duke gave Richmond a large force of men and boats and, with the cooperation of the Duke of Buckingham who later died for his part in this, he sent the earl to land in England. There was a great storm and contrary winds so he had to return to Dieppe and from there he made his way by land back to Brittany. When he had returned to Brittany, he was anxious not to burden the duke with expenses because he had some five hundred English followers and he was afraid the duke might reach some accord with King Richard which would be to his disadvantage. Indeed negotiations were in progress, so he and his company left without bidding the duke goodbye.

2) Polydore Vergil
(*Vergil*, pp. 155, 201-2, 203-4, 205-6, 207-8)

[Jasper Tudor Earl of Pembroke] sailed into France with his brother's son Henry Earl of Richmond [in 1471], whose chance being to arrive in Brittany he presented himself to Francis the duke there.... The duke received them willingly...

[Henry] Earl of Richmond had prepared an army of 5000 Bretons, and furnished a navy of 15 ships, and now approached his day of departure, who began to sail with a prosperous wind [on 6 October 1483]. But a little while before evening a sudden tempest arose, wherewithal he was so affected that his ships were constrained by a cruel gale of wind to turn their course from one way to another; divers of them were blown back into Normandy, others into Brittany. The ship wherein Henry was, with one other, tossed all night long with the waves, came at the last very early in the morning, when the wind grew calm, upon the south coast [at] the haven called Poole. From hence Earl Henry, viewing afar off all the shore beset with soldiers which King Richard had everywhere disposed, [and seeing] none of his own ships within view, hoisted up sail and with prosperous wind came into Normandy.... Here [he] determined to return with part of his retinue on foot into Brittany, and in the meantime sent ambassadors to demand of Charles VIII, King of France, leave to pass through Normandy. The King, pitying the earl's fortune, did not only grant him passage with goodwill but also money to bear his charges...

[After being joined by Thomas Grey Marquis of Dorset and other exiles] Henry upon oath promised that as soon as he should become king [of England] he would marry Elizabeth, King Edward's daughter.... When this was done Earl Henry reported all to the Duke [of Brittany] and prayed him heartily to aid him with more ample supply that he might return forthwith into his country.... The duke promised him aid...

[In England] by the authority of parliament a peace was made with the Scots, who a little before had run furrows about the borders...

[Richard III, in the autumn of 1484, sent ambassadors to the Duke of Brittany but] they could not deal this matter with the duke, for that he had become feeble by reason of sore and daily sickness; wherefore Peter Landofe [Pierre Landais] his treasurer, a man both of sharp wit and great authority, ruled all matters as himself wished, who for that cause had stirred up grievously against himself the envy of the British [Breton] nobility. This man did the English ambassadors deal with, and, explaining their commission, besought him earnestly [to] fulfil King Richard's daily desire [to rid himself of the threat of Henry Tudor]. Peter, who was in great hatred of his own countrymen, supposing that if he should satisfy King Richard he should be more mighty against his adversaries, answered that he would do the thing which King Richard required ... [However] while many messengers and often letters did fly to and fro between Peter and the king, John Bishop of Ely, who lived in Flanders, being certified of that practice from his friends out of England, gave intelligence to Henry forthwith of the plot that was laid [and] advised the earl that he should get himself and the other noble men as soon as he might out of Brittany into France...

[The Duke of Brittany], taking it in evil part that Henry was so uncourteously entertained that he was forced to flee out of his dominion, [laid] the blame of that offence [on Peter], and commanded [that] all Englishmen [he conducted] to the earl. And so Earl Henry, having received all his retinue, was wondrous glad.... King Charles [VIII] promised him aid, and had him be of good cheer, for he would willingly show his goodwill...

3) Crowland Chronicle
(*Crowland*, pp. 171, 173)

... at that time [spring 1484] there was a rumour that the exiles who had been attainted would shortly land in England together with their leader, the Earl of Richmond, to whom all the outcasts, in the hope that a marriage would be contracted with King Edward's daughter, had sworn fealty, as to their king. The king was better prepared to resist them in that year than at any time afterwards, not only because of the treasure which he had in hand—since what King Edward had left behind had not yet all been consumed—but also because of the specific grants made and scattered throughout the kingdom. He observed the new method, introduced by King Edward, at the time of the last war with Scotland, of allocating one mounted courier to every 20 miles; riding with the utmost skill... these men carried messages 200 miles within two days without fail by letters passed from hand to hand. Moreover, he had provided himself with spies overseas... from whom he had learned almost all the movements of his enemies.

In addition, when concerned with maritime affairs right at the beginning of the second year of his reign, although he had lost to the French some ships and two of the toughest captains Sir Thomas Everingham and John Nesfield Esquire, near the town and castle of Scarborough, at the same time and in the same maritime theatre he had remarkable success against the Scots. So considerable was this that they sent the most noble petitioners who could be found in the kingdom as ambassadors to the king at Nottingham town and castle on 7 September [1484], earnestly asking for peace and an end to the fighting in a long and eloquent address—notwithstanding that on land in that same summer, after they had incurred great destruction from our men, they inflicted no less destruction upon us, for the Scottish fugitives, Lord James Douglas and many others who were his companions in exile, besides many Englishmen captured in battle, fell into their hands. Agreements were therefore drawn up, as the king desired, between the commissioners of each kingdom on those matters which seemed to require particular attention...

[On 6 January 1485 the king] was informed by his naval spies that... without any doubt his enemies would invade the kingdom or make an attempt as soon as summer came...

4) Christ Church Letters, Thomas Langton Bishop of St David's to the Prior of Christ Church, September 1483
(Hanham, *Richard III and his Early Historians 1483–1535*, p. 50)

The King of Scots has sent a courteous and a wise letter to the king for peace, but I trow ye shall understand they shall have a sit-up before ever the king depart from York. They lie still at the siege of Dunbar, but I trust to God it shall be kept from them.

5) Richard III to English country gentry, 18 February 1484
(*The North of England in the Age of Richard III*, ed. A. J. Pollard, p. 131)

... we be fully determined, by God's grace, to address us in person with host royal towards the party of our enemies and rebels of Scotland, at the beginning of this next summer.... We charge you [that] you dispose you to serve us personally in the said voyage, accompanied and apparelled for the war, according to your degree.

6) Harleian Manuscript 433
(*Harleian MS 433*, Vol. 3, pp. 105-7)

a) *James III of Scotland to Richard III, 21 July 1484*

... we are now advertised [that] you are inclined to the good of truce and the abstinence of war between our realms, and also that love, amity and alliance of marriage [be] concluded. Whereunto we are likewise inclined. [We therefore ordain] our trusty and well beloved cousins and councillors [Colin Campbell] Earl of Argyll, [John Stewart Lord] Lorne our chancellor, William Bishop of Aberdeen... and Archibald Whitelaw [our] secretary, with full power and commission to come [to] your town of Nottingham on 7 September next...

b) *Richard III to James III, 7 August 1484*

... your loving disposition is to us right agreeable, trusting that by the means of your embassy... such good ways shall be taken between both [our] realms, whereby effusion of Christian blood may be eschewed, love and tenderness grow daily...

7) Archibald Whitelaw's Address to Richard III, 12 September 1484
(*The North of England in the Age of Richard III*, ed. A. J. Pollard, pp. 194-8)

... I make my address before you, in the name and on behalf of my most serene Prince, the King of Scots, who loves you, and who strives for a close friendship and alliance with you...

Most serene Prince, it is the purpose of our embassy and mission that, with the Kings of England and Scotland joined in mutual love, affection, friendship and affinity, their subjects should enjoy the blessings and pleasures of peace and tranquillity...

Most serene Prince, for a long time your subjects, who live within the borders of your realm, in their arrogance preferred war to peace; but now that they see their land lying uncultivated because of war they praise peace and condemn war and battles. They call you to brotherly love with your most noble Prince, it is a love which the nobles of your kingdom, in their wisdom and virtue, demand too. For there has been enough fighting, enough wrongdoing, enough Christian bloodshed in this most recent conflict—in which those who planned the death of all good men and the destruction of peace by force of arms, were immediately overwhelmed and put to flight, and now pay the penalty for their disturbance of the peace, suffering an exile which is worse even than death.... Let every prince be content with the limits, bounds and confines of his own kingdom...

Countless benefits will arise from the love of your people and ours, in union, sweet marriage, matrimony and kinship...

13

HENRY TUDOR EARL OF RICHMOND, THE BATTLE OF BOSWORTH AND THE END OF RICHARD III

During the course of his short reign Richard III made considerable efforts not only to bind his northern followers more closely to him by the judicious exercise of patronage but also significantly widen the basis of his support. Yet, in the end, minor risings in England in 1484-5 and the growing threat of invasion from abroad served to make him *more* rather than less dependent on his existing affinity by the summer of 1485: indeed, according to Rosemary Horrox, when he at last faced his rival on the battlefield early in the morning of 22 August, he was backed very largely by the same men who had helped bring him to power two years previously. Even so, he had good reason to feel confident of success when the crunch came and, at Bosworth, he must have had much the more powerful force, albeit not the colossal numbers suggested by Jean de Molinet (4).

Henry Tudor Earl of Richmond's position, by contrast, had never looked strong: an exile on the Continent since 1471, not only had his expectations of Buckingham's rebellion in October 1483 come to nothing but also, in the autumn of 1484, he had only escaped seizure in Brittany by the very skin of his teeth. By August 1485 his prospects had certainly improved: he had been joined by a steady stream of exiles from England; he had reason to expect (once he landed) military assistance from Thomas Lord Stanley and his brother Sir William (and, perhaps, Henry Percy Earl of Northumberland as well); and, most importantly, he had won the no doubt carefully calculated backing of Charles VIII of France. Although Polydore Vergil suggests that, when he set sail, it was very much on his own initiative and 'with 2000 only of armed men and a few ships', Continental sources such as Philippe de Commines point to his having at least 3,000, if not 4,000, men with him (3). Apart from about 400 English exiles, moreover, most of these were probably professional and experienced French soldiers, a fact underlined by the Crowland continuator's reference to John de Vere Earl of Oxford's having 'a large force of French as well as English troops' at Bosworth fighting for Henry Tudor (1). Nevertheless, when Richmond finally mounted his 'enterprise of England', the memory of his earlier and abortive invasion of October 1483 can hardly have provided a reassuring precedent.

Certainly, in the spring and summer of 1485, there is considerable evidence of Richard III's careful preparations to resist an invasion and, although intelligence reports of Henry Tudor's intended landing at Milford on the south coast proved erroneous (he actually came ashore at Milford Haven in Pembrokeshire on 7 August), the king was nevertheless nicely positioned at Nottingham for an effective response to the Tudor threat (1, 5, 7). As soon as he heard of Henry's arrival, probably on 11 August, Richard summoned his leading supporters to muster their forces and meet him at Leicester where he himself arrived on 19 August (1, 5, 8b). Despite well-founded suspicions regarding the loyalty of the Stanleys (which he vainly tried to counter) and distinctly ominous premonitions as to the outcome of the action, Richard III confronted his rival on the field of Bosworth on 22 August (1).

Although several reports of the ensuing battle have come down to us, most (even the nicely detailed discussion in Polydore Vergil) raise as many problems as they solve, frequently contradict each other and certainly fail to provide either a comprehensive or convincing portrayal of precisely what happened (1, 2, 4, 5, 6, 9, 10). Even the site of the battle was disputed until recently when painstaking archaeological work showed that it was about a mile south west of Ambion Hill, the traditional site of the battle. It seems likely that in the final analysis Richard lost because of the battle tactics employed by the Earl of Oxford, Henry's commander, and the presence of professional French soldiers trained in tactics employed on the continent, as argued by Michael Jones. Richard must, on paper at least, have had a clear advantage in terms of numbers although unfortunately for him Henry Percy, Earl of Northumberland and his no doubt powerful northern contingent never became engaged. Finally Sir William Stanley betrayed his king at the end of the battle after Richard had made a cavalry charge which nearly succeeded in reaching Henry Tudor himself. Richard was killed in the final moments of the battle, probably by a halberd blow to his head which sliced away part of his skull. His body was taken to Leicester where, after probable exposure in the church of St Mary in the Newark for a brief time, he was buried in the Greyfriars, the church of the Franciscans. (1, 4, 5, 6, 10). Even generally hostile sources such as the Crowland continuator and John Rous (1, 2) comment on Richard's courage, and the treatment of his dead body certainly reflects ill on the victor (4, 5, 6). Nevertheless, Henry Tudor had indeed triumphed and, although many northerners may have fought bravely for Richard III (some losing their lives on the field) and the city of York at least mourned his passing (8d), many more may not have been there at all (if only because they failed to make it in time). Even of those who were present, if we are to believe the Crowland chronicler, many 'fled even before coming to blows with the enemy', while substantial numbers too, no doubt, remained aloof from the action in Northumberland's non-participating force on the periphery. Perhaps, indeed, what finally proved fatal to the Yorkist dynasty was not so much Richard III's military errors or his failure to win significant southern backing but a partial collapse of the northern loyalty that had for so long proved his greatest strength.

1) Crowland Chronicle
(*Crowland*, pp. 177, 179, 181, 183)

... rumours grew daily that those in rebellion against the king were making haste and speeding up plans for their invasion of England: the king, however, being in doubt as to where they intended to land... took himself off to the North shortly before Whitsuntide [1485]. Lord Lovell, his chamberlain, was left near Southampton, there to deploy his fleet carefully so as to keep a faithful watch on all the ports of those parts and not to miss the chance of engaging the enemy with the united forces of the whole neighbourhood if they tried to land there.

As a result of this unnecessary policy, stores and money were lost there.... Some say there is a port called Milford in the neighbourhood of Southampton as well as one in Wales. And because some people, as though gifted with the spirit of prophecy, foretold that these men would land at

the port of Milford... the king saw fit to set up many forts, at this time, in that southern part of the kingdom. It was in vain. On August 1, with a favourable breeze, they landed at the well-known port of Milford near Pembroke without opposition.

When he heard of their arrival the king rejoiced, or at least he pretended to rejoice, sending his letters everywhere to say that the day he had longed for had now arrived when he could easily triumph over such a wretched company.... Meanwhile he sent out terrifying orders in manifold letters to all the counties of the kingdom: none of their men [of property] should withdraw themselves from the coming battle, with the threat that, after victory had been gained, anyone who might be found, in any part of the kingdom, not to have been present in person with him on the battlefield could hope for nothing but the loss of all his goods, his possessions and his life.

A little before the arrival of these men, Thomas Stanley, steward of the king's household, received permission to go across to Lancashire, his native country, to see his home and family from whom he had long been away. He was not allowed to make any long stay there, unless he sent his first-born son George Lord Strange to the king at Nottingham, which he did.

[The king's opponents] made their way along wild and twisting tracks in the north [of Wales], where William Stanley, brother of the same lord steward and chamberlain of north Wales, was in sole command. The king then sent orders to Lord [Thomas] Stanley to present himself before the king at Nottingham without any delay. The king feared—what in fact happened—that the Earl of Richmond's mother, who was the wife of Lord Stanley, might induce her husband to support her son's party. [He] was not able to come [he alleged because of] the sweating sickness from which he was suffering.... However, his son, who had secretly prepared to escape from the king, was discovered by a snare and seized; he revealed a conspiracy to support the party of the Earl of Richmond between himself, his uncle, William Stanley, and Sir John Savage, asked for mercy and promised that his father would come to the king's aid, as fast as possible, with all his power. In addition he wrote to his father announcing the danger he was in together with the urgent need of presenting help of this sort.

Meanwhile... the enemy was making haste and moving by day and night towards a direct confrontation with the king and therefore it was necessary to move the army, though it was not yet fully assembled, away from Nottingham, and to proceed to Leicester. On the king's side there was a greater number of fighting men than had ever been seen before, on the one side, in England. [On 22 August] the king left Leicester with great pomp, wearing his diadem on his head, and accompanied by John Howard Duke of Norfolk and Henry Percy Earl of Northumberland, and other great lords, knights and esquires, and a countless multitude of commoners...

The chief men in the opposing army were these: firstly, Henry Earl of Richmond, whom they called their king, Henry VII; John Vere Earl of Oxford; John Lord Welles, uncle of King Henry VII; Thomas Lord Stanley and his brother William; Edward Woodville... and many others notable for their military standing.... There were present also counsellors who were churchmen and who had likewise endured exile...

At dawn on Monday morning the chaplains were not ready to celebrate mass for King Richard nor was any breakfast ready with which to revive the king's flagging spirit. The king, so it was reported, had seen that night, in a terrible dream, a multitude of demons apparently surrounding him, just as he attested in the morning when he presented a countenance which was always drawn but was then even more pale and deathly, and affirmed that the outcome of this day's battle, to whichever side the victory was granted, would totally destroy the kingdom of England. For he also declared that he would ruin all the partisans of the other side, if he emerged as the victor, predicting that his adversary would do exactly the same to the king's supporters if the victory fell to him. Finally... he ordered that Lord Strange should be beheaded on the spot. However, those to whom this task was given, seeing that the matter in hand was at a very critical stage and that it was more important than the elimination of one man, failed to carry out that king's cruel command...

There now began a very fierce battle between the two sides: the Earl of Richmond, with his knights, advanced directly upon King Richard, while the Earl of Oxford ... with a large force of French as well as English troops took up his position opposite ... the Duke of Norfolk.... In the place where the earl of Northumberland stood, with a fairly large and well-equipped force, there was no contest against the enemy and no blows given or received in battle. In the end a glorious victory was granted by heaven to the Earl of Richmond.... As for King Richard, he received many mortal wounds, and like a spirited and most courageous prince, fell in the battle and not in flight. The Duke of Norfolk, Sir Richard Ratcliffe, Sir Robert Brackenbury ... and many others were killed in that frenzy of battle; and many northerners, in whom, especially, King Richard placed so much trust, fled even before coming to blows with the enemy.... Out of this warfare came peace for the whole kingdom, and King Richard's body having been discovered among the dead ... many other insults were offered ... [Many] noblemen and others were captured, in particular Henry Earl of Northumberland and Thomas Howard Earl of Surrey ... William Catesby... pre-eminent among all the counsellors of the late king was also captured; as a final reward for excellent service his head was cut off at Leicester.

2) John Rous
(Hanham, *Richard III and his Early Historians 1483–1535*, pp. 123-4)

... as the life of King Richard approached its evening, many secretly left him and joined the exiles from the south who were with Henry Earl of Richmond.... And like the Antichrist to come, he was confounded at his moment of greatest pride. For having with him the crown itself, together with great quantities of treasure, he was unexpectedly cut down in the midst of his army by an invading army small by comparison but furious in impetus, like a wretched creature. For all that, let me say the truth to his credit: that he bore himself like a gallant knight and, despite his little body and feeble strength, honourably defended himself to his last breath, shouting again and again that he was betrayed, and crying 'Treason! Treason!'. So, tasting what he had often administered to others, he ended his life most miserably, and finally was buried in the choir of the Friars Minor at Leicester. Although his days were short, they were ended with no lamentation from his groaning subjects.

3) Philippe de Commines
(*Commines*, pp. 355, 397-8)

[Henry Tudor Earl of Richmond] was paid just enough money for the passage of 3 or 4000 men. The present king [Charles VIII] gave those who were with him a large sum of money and some artillery. He was taken by ship from Normandy to land in his native Wales. King Richard marched to meet him, but the Earl of Richmond was joined by Lord Stanley, an English knight and husband of the earl's mother, with reinforcements numbering more than 26,000 men. A battle was fought. King Richard was killed on the battlefield and the Earl of Richmond was crowned King of England on the field with Richard's crown...

God suddenly raised up against King Richard an enemy who had neither money, nor rights, so I believe, to the crown of England, nor any reputation except what his own person and honesty brought him. He had suffered much since, for the best part of his life from the age of eighteen, he had been a prisoner in Brittany in the hands of Duke Francis, although he had treated him well for a prisoner. He, with a little money from the king and some 3000 of the most unruly men that could be found and enlisted in Normandy, crossed over to Wales where he was joined by his father-in-law, Lord Stanley, and a good 25,000 Englishmen. After three or four days they encountered cruel King Richard. He was killed on the battlefield. Henry was crowned and he is still ruling today.

4) Jean de Molinet
(Bennett, *The Battle of Bosworth*, p. 161)

King Richard... had around 60,000 combatants and a great number of cannons. The leader of the vanguard was Lord John Howard.... Another lord, Brackenbury, [was] also in command of the van, which had 11,000 or 12,000 altogether.... The French also made their preparations marching against the English...

The king had the artillery of his army fire on the Earl of Richmond, and so the French, knowing by the king's shot the lie of the land and the order of his battle, resolved, in order to avoid the fire, to mass their troops against the flank rather than the front of the king's battle. Thus they obtained the mastery of his vanguard...

The vanguard of King Richard, which was put to flight, was picked off by Lord Stanley who, with all of 20,000 combatants, came at a good pace to the aid of the earl. The Earl of Northumberland, who was on the king's side with 10,000 men, ought to have charged the French, but did nothing except to flee, both he and his company, and to abandon his King Richard, for he had an undertaking with the Earl of Richmond, as had some others who deserted him in his need. The king bore himself valiantly... and bore the crown on his head; but, when he saw this discomfiture and found himself alone on the field, he thought to run after the others. His horse leapt into a marsh from which it could not retrieve itself. One of the Welshmen then came after him, and struck him dead with a halberd, and another took his body and put it before him on his horse and carried it, hair hanging as one would bear a sheep.

And so he who had miserably killed numerous people ended his days iniquitously and filthily in the dirt and mire, and he who had despoiled churches was displayed to the people naked and without any clothing, and without royal solemnity was buried at the entrance to a village church.

5) Great Chronicle of London
(*Great Chronicle*, pp. 237-8)

... true knowledge came to the king at the beginning of August of the landing of Prince Henry... at Milford Haven in Wales...

Then King Richard in all haste arrayed his people and made quick provision to meet his enemies which, at the beginning, were but of small strength. But, as soon as his landing was known to many of the knights and esquires of this land, they gathered many people in the king's name and straight sped them unto that other party, by means whereof his power hugely increased.

Then King Richard, being well accompanied, sped towards his enemies till he came to Leicester, and that other party, which meanwhile had proclaimed himself King Henry VII, drew fast thitherward. But that night King Richard lost many of his people, for many gentlemen that held good countenance with master Brackenbury, then lieutenant of the Tower, and had for many of them done right kindly, took their leave of him, giving him thanks for his kindness, and exhorted him to go with them, for they feared not to show him that they would go unto that other party, and so departed, leaving him almost alone.

Meanwhile the Earl of Derby and the Earl of Northumberland, who had each of them great companies, made slow speed towards King Richard, so that he with the Duke of Norfolk and the Earl of Surrey, Lord Lovell and others, departed from Leicester with great triumph and pomp upon the morn being the 22 August, and after continued his journey till he came to a village called Bosworth where, in the fields adjoining, both hosts met, and fought there a sharp and long fight whereof in the end the victory fell to King Henry. In this battle were slain King Richard, the Duke of Norfolk, the Lord Lovell, with Brackenbury and many others. And incontinently, as it was said, Sir William Stanley, who won the possession of King Richard's helmet with the crown being upon it, came straight to King Henry and set it upon his head saying, 'Sir, here I make you King of England' ...

And thus by great fortune and grace... won this noble prince the possession of this land, and then was he conveyed to Leicester the same night, and there received with all honour and gladness.

And Richard late king, [his] body despoiled to the skin and nought being left about him so much as would cover his privy member, was trussed behind a pursuivant called Norroy as a hog or other vile beast, and so, all bespattered with mire and filth, was brought to a church in Leicester for all men to wonder upon, and there lastly irreverently buried.

6) Polydore Vergil
(*Vergil*, pp. 223-6)

[At the battle of Bosworth] the number of all [Henry Tudor's] soldiers, altogether, was scarcely 5000, beside the Stanleyans, of whom about 3000 were at the battle, under the conduct of William.... The king's forces were twice as many and more.

... Henry bore the brunt [of the fighting] longer than even his own soldiers would have thought, who were now almost out of hope of victory, when, behold, William Stanley with 3000 men came to the rescue; then truly in a very moment the residue all fled, and King Richard alone was killed fighting manfully in the thickest press of his enemies. In the meantime also the Earl of Oxford, after a little skirmishing, put to flight those that fought in the forward, whereof a great company were killed in the chase. But many more forebore to fight, who came to the field with King Richard for awe, and for no goodwill and departed without any danger, as men who desired not the safety but destruction of that prince whom they hated.

There were killed about 1000 men, and amongst them [were] John Duke of Norfolk, Walter Lord Ferrers, Robert Brackenbury, Richard Ratcliffe and many more. Two days after at Leicester, William Catesby, lawyer, with a few that were his fellows, were executed. And of those who took to their feet Francis Lord Lovell, Humphrey Stafford, with Thomas his brother and much more company, fled into sanctuary.... As for the number of captives, it was very great; for when King Richard was killed, all men forthwith threw away weapon and freely submitted themselves to Henry's obedience, whereof the most part would have done the same at the beginning [but] for King Richard's scouts.... Amongst them the chief were Henry Earl of Northumberland and Thomas Earl of Surrey.... Henry lost in that battle scarcely a hundred soldiers...

The report is that King Richard might have sought to save himself by flight; for they who were about him, seeing the soldiers even from the first stroke to lift up their weapons feebly and faintly, and some of them to depart the field privily, suspected treason, and exhorted him to fly, and when the matter began manifestly to falter, they brought him swift horses; but he, who was not ignorant that the people hated him, [is] said to have answered that that very day he would make an end either of war or life...

Henry, after the victory obtained, gave forthwith thanks unto Almighty God for the same... [The] soldiers cried, 'God save King Henry, God save King Henry!', and with heart and hand uttered all the show of joy that might be; which, when Thomas Stanley did see, he set at once King Richard's crown, which was found among the spoil in the field, upon his head...

[The] body of King Richard, naked of all clothing, and laid upon a horse's back, with the arms and legs hanging down on both sides, was brought to the abbey of Franciscan monks at Leicester, a miserable spectacle in good truth, but not unworthy for the man's life, and there was buried two days after without any pomp or solemn funeral.

7) Richard III's Proclamation against Henry Tudor, 23 June 1485
(*Paston Letters*, Vol. 6, pp. 81-2, 84)

Forasmuch as the king our sovereign lord has certain knowledge that Peter, Bishop of Exeter, Jasper Tudor ... calling himself Earl of Pembroke, John late Earl of Oxford, and Sir Edward Woodville, and diverse others his rebels and traitors... have forsaken their natural country, breaking them first to be under the obedience of the Duke of Brittany, and have promised to him certain things which he and his council thought were too greatly unnatural and abominable for them to grant... and therefore utterly refused the same.

The said traitors [then] privily departed out of his country into France, and there betook them to be under the obedience of the king's ancient enemy, Charles, calling himself king of France; and in order to abuse and blind the commons of this realm, these rebels and traitors have chosen to be their captain Henry Tudor... who of his ambition and insatiable covetousness encroaches and usurps unto him the name and title of royal estate of this realm of England...

[The king commands] all his subjects to be ready in their most defensible array to do his highness service of war... for the resistance of the king's rebels, traitors and enemies...

8) York Civic Records
(*York Civic Records*, Vol. 1, pp. 117, 118, 119)

a) *16 August 1485*

... it was determined that John Sponer, sergeant to the mace, should ride to Nottingham to the king's grace, to understand his pleasure as in sending up any of his subjects within this city to his grace for the subduing of his enemies late arrived in the parts of Wales, or otherwise as it shall be disposed at his most high pleasure.

b) *19 August 1485*

... it was determined... that 80 men of the city, defensibly arrayed, John Hastings, gentleman to the mace, being captain, should in all haste possible depart towards the king's grace for the subduing of his enemies...

c) *23 August 1485*

... on 22 day of August 1485, at Redmoor near Leicester, there was fought a battle between our lord King Richard III and others of his nobles on the one part and Henry Earl of Richmond and others of his nobles on the other part. In this battle ... John Duke of Norfolk, Thomas Earl of Lincoln, Thomas Earl of Surrey, son of the aforesaid duke, Francis Viscount Lovell, Lord Walter Devereux, Lord Ferrers, Sir Robert Ratcliffe and Sir Robert Brackenbury, the lord king at Sandeford near Leicester, and others in the same field, with many other nobles, knights, esquires and gentlemen were killed.

d) *23 August 1485*

... it was shown by divers persons, especially by John Sponer sent unto the field of Redmoor to bring tidings from the same to the city, that King Richard, late lawfully reigning over us, was, through great treason of the Duke of Norfolk [sic Northumberland] and many others that turned against him, with many other lords and nobility of these north parts, piteously slain and murdered, to the great heaviness of this city...

9) Diego de Valera to the Catholic Monarchs of Castile and Aragon, 1 March 1486
(Tudor-Craig, *Richard III*, p. 68)

... in spite of his being a powerful monarch, sole ruler in his kingdom without any contradiction, our Lord did not permit [King Richard's] evil deeds to remain unpunished, but rather put a new heart in the Earl of Richmond, Henry by name, who was in Brittany, an exile and in poor enough estate, and to whom the realm lawfully belonged, with the result that he went to the king of France begging counsel, favour and assistance. The latter… granted him 2000 combatants paid for four months, and lent him 50,000 crowns, and gave him his fleet in which to make passage, [and] with these aids and 3000 Englishmen whom he found in France that had fled from King Richard. He crossed into England and entered by way of Wales, conquering all positions as he progressed as far as a town called Coventry, near which King Richard stood in the field with as many as 70,000 combatants. But… previous to his entry into England, he had the assurance that my Lord Tamorlant, one of the principal nobles of England, and sundry other leading men, who had given him their oath and seals, would give him assistance when they came to battle and would fight against King Richard, and so they did. Though his people came with a faint heart, as not knowing the secret but fully aware of the multitude of King Richard's army, he greatly heartened them to come to the battlefield.

When King Richard was certified of the near approach of Earl Henry in battle array, he ordered his lines and entrusted the van to his grand chamberlain with 7000 fighting men. My Lord Tamorlant with King Richard's left wing left his position and passed in front of the king's vanguard with 10,000 men, then, turning his back on Earl Henry, he began to fight fiercely against the king's van, and so did all the others who had plighted their faith to Earl Henry. Now when Salazar, your little vassal, who was there in King Richard's service, saw the treason of the king's people, he went up to him and said, 'Sire, take steps to put your person in safety, without expecting to have the victory in today's battle, owing to the manifest treason in your following'. But the king replied: 'Salazar, God forbid I yield one step. This day I will die as a king or win'. Then he placed over his head-armour the crown royal [and] having donned his coat of arms began to fight with much vigour, putting heart into those that remained loyal, so that by his sole effort he upheld the battle for a long time. But in the end the king's army was beaten and he himself killed, and in this battle above 10,000 men are said to have perished on both sides. Salazar fought bravely, but for all this was able to escape. There died most of those who loyally served the king, and there was lost all the king's treasure, which he brought with him into the field.

After winning this victory, Earl Henry was at once acclaimed king by all parties. He ordered the dead king to be placed in a little hermitage near the place of battle, and had him covered from the waist downward with a black rag of poor quality, ordering him to be exposed there three days to the universal gaze.

10) Ballad of Bosworth Field
(*Bishop Percy's Folio Manuscript*, Vol. 3, pp. 237-8, 256-7)

... at Milford Haven, when he did appear
With all his lords in royal array,
He said to them that with him were:
'Into England I am entered here,
My heritage is this land within;
They shall me boldly bring and bear,
And lose my life, but I'll be king...
Send me the love of the Lord Stanley!
He married my mother...
And his brother Sir William, the good Stanley...
A more nobler knight at need
Came never to maintain king.'
Now leave we Henry, this prince royal,
And talk of Richard in his dignity,
Of the great misfortune did him befall:
The causer of his own death was he...
King Richard did in his army stand,
He was numbered to 40000 and 3
Of hardy men of heart and hand,
That under his banner there did be.
Sir William Stanley wise and worthy...
Down at a back then cometh he,
And shortly set upon the king.
Then they countered together sad and sore;
Archers they let sharp arrows flee...
Then our archers let their shooting be...
There died many a doughty knight...
Thus they fought with main and might
That was on Henry's part, our king.
Then to King Richard there came a knight,
And said, 'I hold it time for to flee...'
[Richard] said, 'Give me my battle-axe in my hand,
Set the crown of England on my head so high!
For by Him that shape both sea and land,
King of England this day I will die!'

BIBLIOGRAPHY

Bennett, Michael, *The Battle of Bosworth* (Gloucester, 1985)

Bishop Percy's Folio Manuscript, ed. J. W. Hales and F. J. Furnivall, Vol. 3 (London, 1868)

British Library Harleian Manuscript 433, ed. R. Horrox and P. W. Hammond, 4 vols (Richard III Society, 1979-83)

Buck, Sir George, *The History of King Richard III*, ed. A. N. Kincaid (Gloucester, 1982)

Calendar of Patent Rolls, Edward IV, 1467-77, Edward IV–Edward V–Richard III, 1476–85 (1899, 1901)

Chronicles of London, ed. C. L. Kingsford (1905, reprinted Gloucester, 1977)

Commynes, Philippe de, *Memoirs: The Reign of Louis XI 1461-83*, transl. M. Jones (London, 1972)

Crowland Chronicle Continuations 1459–1486, ed. N. Pronay and J. Cox (Gloucester, 1986)

Dockray, K. R., (Headstart History pamphlet, 1992)

England under the Yorkists 1460–1485, ed. I. D. Thornley (London, 1920)

English Historical Documents, IV, 1327–1485, ed. A. R. Myers (London, 1969)

Fabyan, Robert, *The New Chronicles of England and of France*, ed. H. Ellis (London, 1811)

Gairdner, James, *History of the Life and Reign of Richard the Third* (2nd edn, Cambridge, 1898)

Great Chronicle of London, ed. A. H. Thomas and I. D. Thornley (1938, reprinted Gloucester, 1983)

Green, J. R., *A Short History of the English People* (London, 1874)

Green, R. F., 'Historical Notes of a London Citizen 1483-1488', *English Historical Review*, Vol. 96 (1981)

Hall, Edward, *The Union of the Two Noble Families of Lancaster and York* (1550, reprinted Scolar Press, 1970)

Halsted, Caroline A., *Richard III as Duke of Gloucester and King of England*, 2 vols (1844, reprinted Gloucester, 1977)

Hammond, P. W. and Sutton, A. F., *Richard III: The Road to Bosworth Field* (London, 1985)

Hanham, Alison, *Richard III and his Early Historians 1483-1535* (Oxford, 1975)

Hicks, M. A., *Richard III: The Man Behind the Myth* (London, 1991)

Historie of the Arrivall of Edward IV in England, ed. J. Bruce (Camden Society, 1838)

Holinshed's Chronicle, ed. A. and J. Nicholl (London, 1927)

Horrox, R., *Richard III: A Study of Service* (Cambridge, 1989)

Kendall, Paul Murray, *Richard the Third* (London, 1955)

Lindsay, Philip, *King Richard III* (London, 1933)

Lingard, John, *The History of England from the first invasion by the Romans to the accession of William and Mary in 1688*, 3 vols (London, 1819)

Mancini, Dominic, *The Usurpation of Richard III*, ed. and trans. C. A. J. Armstrong (Oxford 1969, reprinted Gloucester, 1984)

Markham, Sir Clements R., *Richard III: His Life and Character* (London 1906, reprinted Bath, 1973)

More, Sir Thomas, *The History of King Richard III*, ed. R. S. Sylvester (Complete Works, Yale edn, 11, 1963)

Myers, A. R. 'The Character of Richard III', *History Today*, iv (1954), reprinted in *English Society and Government in the Fifteenth Century*, ed. C. M. D. Crowder, London, 1967)

Myers, A. R., 'Richard III and Historical Tradition', *History*, liii (1968)

Paston Letters 1422–1509, ed. J. Gairdner, 6 vols (1904, reprinted Gloucester, in one volume, 1983)

Plumpton Correspondence, ed. T. Stapleton (Camden Society 1839, reprinted Gloucester, 1990)

Pollard, A. J., *North Eastern England during the Wars of the Roses* (Oxford, 1990)

Pollard, A. J., *Richard III and the Princes in the Tower* (Stroud, 1991)

Pollard, A. J. (ed.), *The North of England in the Age of Richard III* (Stroud, 1996)

Potter, Jeremy, *Good King Richard?* (London, 1983)

Richard III. A Medieval Kingship, ed. J. Gillingham (London, 1993)

Richmond, Colin, '1485 and All That, or what was going on at the Battle of Bosworth?' in *Richard III: Loyalty, Lordship and Law*, ed. P. W. Hammond (London, 1986)

Ross, Charles, *Edward IV* (London, 1974)

Ross, Charles, *Richard III* (London, 1981)

Rotuli Parliamentorum, ed. J. Strachey and others, 6 vols (1767–77)

Rous, John, *The Rous Roll* (1859, reprinted Gloucester, 1980)

Rous, John, *The History of the Kings of England*, in A. Hanham, *Richard III and his Early Historians 1483–1535* (Oxford, 1975)

Rowse, A. L., Bosworth Field and the Wars of the Roses (London, 1966)

Sandford, Francis, A Genealogical History of the Kings and Queens of England (2nd edn, London, 1707)

Seward, Desmond, *Richard III: England's Black Legend* (London, 1983)

Shakespeare, William, *King Richard III*, ed. A. Hammond (London, 1981) Statutes of the Realm, 1101-1713 (Record Commission, 1810-28)

Stonor Letters and Papers 1290–1483, ed. C. L. Kingsford, 2 vols (Camden Society, 1919)

Stubbs, William, *The Constitutional History of England*, 3 vols (Oxford, 1878)

Tey, Josephine, *The Daughter of Time* (London, 1951)

Tudor-Craig, Pamela, *Richard III* (London, 1973)

Turner, Sharon, *The History of England during the Middle Ages*, 3 vols (3rd edn, London, 1830)

Vergil, Polydore, *Three Books of Polydore Vergil's English History*, ed. H. Ellis (Camden Society, 1844)

Walpole, Horace, *Historic Doubts on the Life and Reign of Richard III*, ed. P. W. Hammond (Gloucester, 1987)

Warkworth, John, *A Chronicle of the First Thirteen Years of the Reign of King Edward the Fourth*, ed. J. O. Halliwell (Camden Society, 1839)

Wood, C. T., *Joan of Arc* (Oxford, 1988)

York Civic Records, Vol. 1, ed. A. Raine (Yorkshire Archaeological Society Record Series, 1939)